Once these European bison or wisent roamed the forests of Europe, but the disappearance of the forests severely reduced their numbers. Only dedicated and timely conservation saved the European bison from extinction.

ANIMALS IN PERIL

Man's War Against Wildlife

ANIMALS IN PERIL

Peter Verney

Brigham Young University Press

For Louisa

© 1979 Peter Verney

Published in Great Britain by
Mills & Boon Ltd, London, England

Published simultaneously in the United States by
Brigham Young University Press, Provo, Utah.

International Standard Book Number: 0–8425–1714–6 (cloth)
Library of Congress Catalog Card Number: 79–2786

Manufactured in Great Britain

Contents

Introduction 12
1 The Great Whale Hunt 14
2 Fur Fever 36
3 The Passing of the Buffalo 60
4 White Gold 82
5 'The Lost Glories of an Abundant Land': Disappearing Birds 102
6 Safari and Shikar: Big Game Hunting 132
7 A Report from the Front 166
8 A New Enlightenment? 174
Acknowledgments 186
Picture Credits 187

Introduction

And God said, 'Let us make man in our image, after our likeness: and let them have dominion over the fish of the sea, and over the fowl of the air, and over the cattle, and over all the earth, and over every creeping thing that creepeth upon the earth.'

GENESIS 1:26

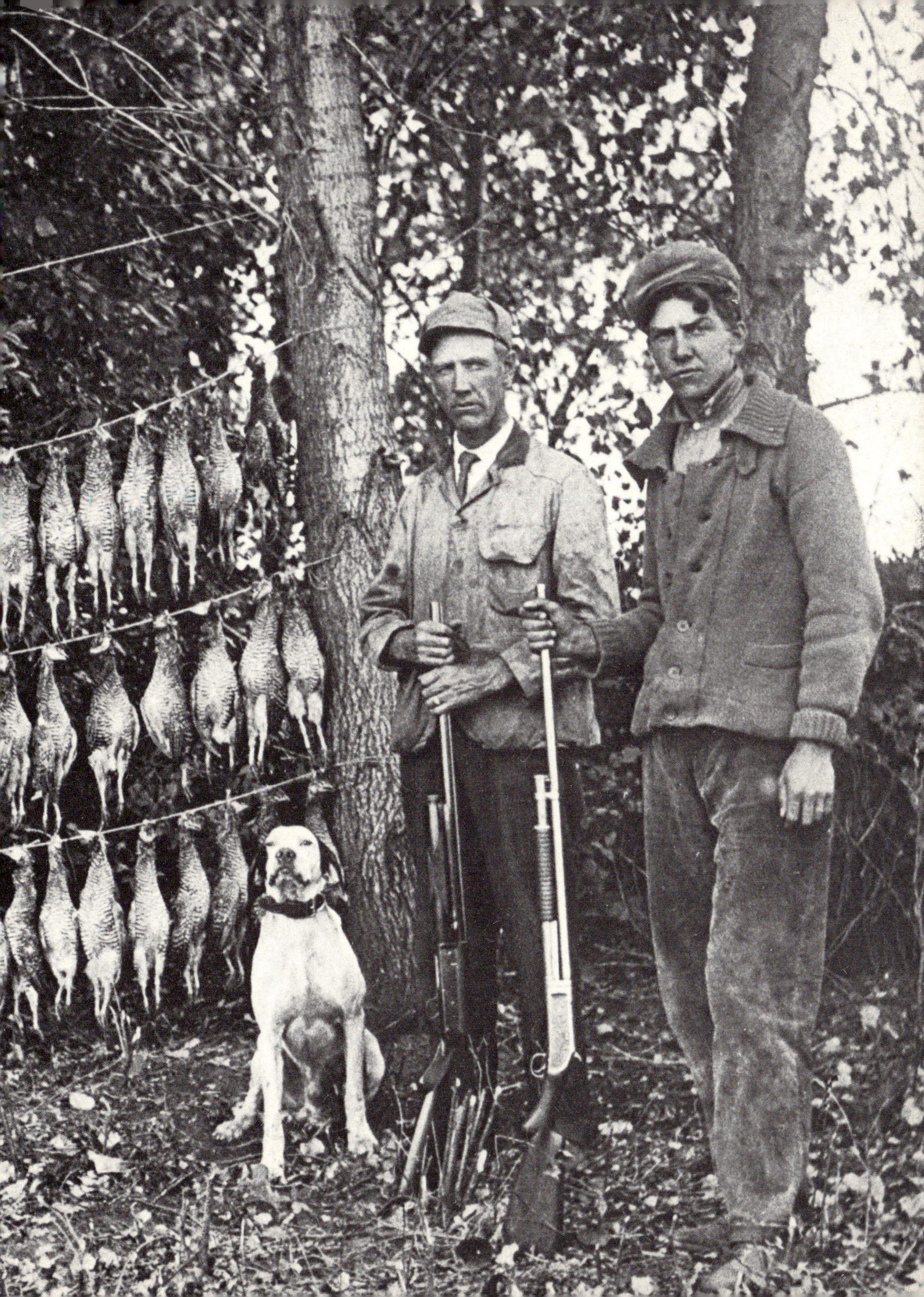

The story of man on earth is one of competition, often of conflict, not only with his own kind but with the animal kingdom and the resources of the natural world. Our primitive ancestors saw wild animals as providing their meat, their clothing and much of the material of their existence. They hunted and killed when the need arose. Sometimes their hunting was wasteful; more often they killed only when they had to and lived in a state of harmony with the creatures around. They lived to hunt and hunted to live and they came to worship and respect the quarry which enabled them to exist at all.

As man the hunter became man the shepherd, then the farmer, and his kind multiplied, he started to encroach on the wild preserves around him. Although these early depredations were sometimes drastic and irreversible, man was later to be a much more effective killer when he could carry a gun. For with the advent of the firearm, *Homo sapiens* truly became *Homo tyrannicus.*

Zoologists are agreed that when man started to make a real impact on his natural world, some species were already on the decline. Too often, however, man's greed and improvidence—often his ignorance also—have accelerated, and in some cases have begun the process of decline. Man has slaughtered animals for use; he has killed some for sport. He has introduced alien species with excellent short-term intentions, and cataclysmic long-term results. He has annihilated predators to the detriment of the herds he sought to protect. He has allowed, even encouraged, over-grazing and the widespread destruction of forests and natural resources, with no thought for the future.

Primitive man was a part of the natural world around him. Even if he feared the dark of the forest and the mystery of the wild he was never in a position to alter the overall balance and his effect on animal life was mostly transient and local. But as modern man started to stretch his frontiers, to multiply at an increasing rate and to improve his technology, so he came to threaten the indigenous animal population and to dominate Nature—and Nature had to give way.

It was some time before man woke to the fact that his depredations had already exterminated some species and threatened the very survival of others. Around a hundred years ago, men first began seriously to ask themselves whether they ever had a moral right to exploit the animal kingdom, and to question whether it was even in their own best interests to do so to the point of extinction. A creeping anxiety over what had occurred began to grow, and with it a realization that something must be done before man's wanton destruction of wildlife and nature would leave nothing on this planet (on which in any case his generation was no more than the sitting tenant) than wasted plains, parched and arid prairies and the memory of animal and plant riches long gone. The conservation movement was born. The effort had come late—in some cases it had come too late—but it was the start of

(Previous pages) The once numerous prairie chickens were almost wiped out due to loss of habitat and excessive hunting in the 1920s and 30s.

the long process of reconciliation between man and the natural world.

The irony is, that over the ages man has been driven forward by the very civilization he has created for himself: he has spun a fine web only to find himself as enmeshed as securely as his prey. Just as the elephant or the rhino if allowed to become too numerous in too small a space will eat down his own habitat until his very survival is threatened, so man makes greater and greater demands on finite natural resources. As stocks dwindle and become scarce so his killing methods have to improve, and history shows that only too often he has been unaware that he was destroying the actual foundations of his own existence and prosperity. Now, after so many words have been spent on the various aspects of exploitation, we are no longer quite sure who was the victim.

There are close parallels between the conquest of the animal kingdom and the colonization of other human societies. Many fascinating mirror images link the two worlds. There is a primary stage in which the aggressor feels an untroubled sense of justification, even of divine right; a secondary stage when minority protest begins to crack the face of public opinion; and a third stage when the full weight of popular feeling swings against the old orthodoxy in a surge of guilt and self-recrimination. With this last stage comes a wondering at the ambivalent attitudes which had characterized the past, and a tendency to sentimentalize the victim in a belated attempt to rectify wrong.

During this final reappraisal and scrutiny we tend to forget *why* things happened as they did: what forces drove the whalers to all but annihilate certain whale species; why the elimination of the buffalo was an essential ingredient in the pacification of the North American Indian; how fashion decided the fate of countless millions of birds towards the turn of the century; even how the search for animal wealth led to the exploration of vast stretches of virgin territory in several continents.

This book is the history of man's long war against the animal world, and I have tried to tell it with the objectivity of a war correspondent. Like all wars much is brutal and brutalizing, but in order to prevent this becoming a catalogue of man's devastation I have also tried to understand the forces—commercial, economic, colonial—that drove him on.

Now we are in a final stage in this war—the Age of Conservation, of caring, of awareness, of education to a true appreciation of our natural heritage. And the war goes on—perhaps not as dramatically as with hand-held harpoons, but as destructively as ever and on a dozen different fronts as we continue our subjugation of the natural world by technology. We can only hope that if some of the past events in the war can be recognized and understood, they will serve as a warning for the present, and a reminder of our obligation to the future.

The Great Whale Hunt

The moot point is, whether Leviathan can long endure so wide a chase, and so remorseless a havoc; whether he must not at last be exterminated from the waters, and the last whale, like the last man, smoke his last pipe, and then himself evaporate in the final puff.

Herman Melville, 1851

An Arctic Panorama (from Bankes's New System of Geography).

The puny boats and hand-held harpoons of the early whalers were no threat to the survival of the whale. Only when man's hunting techniques became more sophisticated, his equipment more deadly and his appetite for whale products so demanding were the great whales placed in jeopardy.

There is no more stark example of the systematic exploitation of a natural resource, no more chilling indictment of man's cupidity, improvidence and short-sightedness. It is a tale of species being slaughtered to the point of extinction, of once-rich hunting grounds being stripped of whale stocks, of a growing threat to the survival of most whales and it has led to increasingly stringent quotas being imposed on the whale-catchers of the world by the International Whaling Commission—whose actions, some think, have come too late and are too lenient.

On many shores throughout the world the providential arrival of a stranded whale provided nourishment for an entire community for months on end and was looked upon as a gift from the gods. In many cultures the strange, incomprehensible whale was granted divine properties, harbingers of good luck, and if a whale became stranded they would do all in their power to set it on its way again. In Norse mythology the 'good' whales were thought of as god-sent. They were clean creatures which fed 'on the darkness and rain that fall onto the sea'. Each year they were relied on to drive the herring shoals close to land and the waiting fishermen.

Catching whales in North America, according to T. de Bry.

Many native communities in various parts of the globe hunted close to their shores and the eskimos in their frail kayaks would hunt down whales basking on the surface and sink stone-headed spears into the sleeping bulk. Plunging mightily to the bottom after this sudden assault, the creature sooner or later died and in a few days, provided the wind and tide were right, the great carcase would drift ashore to be set upon by the delighted hunters. To speed the process the spearheads

To our ancestors, the whale was a mysterious monster of the deep. Description de L'Univers, Allaine Manesson Mallet, 1685.

might be dipped in poison, either taken from the roots of plants such as aconitum or anemone, or else from the juices of rotting meat—for the whale is very susceptible to blood poisoning.

The Japanese also used poison—that from a rich man newly dead and dug up for the occasion was considered highly efficacious when painted on their primitive harpoon points! Others found that nets could also be used to trap whales as they passed on migration, and this form of hunting flourished.

But it was the hardy hunters of the Bay of Biscay, as long ago as the tenth or eleventh century, who are commonly acknowledged to have set in train what was to become a world-wide industry. Their quarry was what became known as the black right whale, (right because it was the 'right' whale to catch from small boats). Relatively slow and some 60 feet long it frequented temperate waters passing on migration through the Bay of Biscay.

To early hunters, though, the great whales were objects of awe and terror. When they blundered into the nets, the infuriated seamen would drive them away with spears and arrows and then, to their great surprise, discovered the huge animals to be inoffensive, almost gentle, despite their vast bulk. Further, they were peculiarly vulnerable to wounding. When first set upon they would plunge to the bottom, but

Cutting up the whale—to musical accompaniment. Illustration by André Thevet from Cosmographie Universelle *1574.*

on inevitable resurfacing, they would often be so exhausted that they could not escape. On many occasions the Biscayans discovered that a single spear thrust to a vital part was enough to wound mortally and later the dead whale would be found swept up on shore.

A further surprise was in store when they learnt of the richness of the whale products. For a single animal would yield enough oil to light their homes for several years, the meat was good to eat, the great bones made fine supports for their houses and their roofs, and in the mouth of the creature was a strange substance with great flexibility and strength, firm on one side, covered with bristles on the other, and with a wealth of different uses—whalebone. From accidental encounters it was not long before the men of the Bay of Biscay started to deliberately hunt the whale.

Spitsbergen. After slaying the whale the carcase was winched ashore for cutting up. After a contemporary print.

When even these insignificant hunting exploits disturbed the whales and drove them from the coastal waters, the Biscayans built larger ships and pursued their quarry across the Atlantic until they found more whales along the Great Banks of Newfoundland, a place teeming with fish of all sorts. But these were small-scale efforts, for their boats could hardly manage the products of more than a single whale, and even when the Biscayans were joined by the Icelanders, there was little strain on the supply despite at one time the combined fleets totalling more than 50 sail.

But it was the lure of the Indies, the search for an alternative route to this treasure-house of the world via the North-West Passage, that first brought European seafarers into contact with the whale-rich waters beyond the Arctic Circle, and those around the islands of Spitsbergen in particular. It was here, in 1610, that the first English whaling expedition ventured, and so successful was the voyage that it was repeated the next year with two rather larger boats, and six Basque harpooners who taught the newcomers their art. After a series of misfortunes both boats foundered but the crews were saved and so were the cargoes which were brought back to England in triumph.

This was the start of what became a seasonal rush to the north each

Whaling in Greenland waters.

year. The English were not left alone for long. Soon the Biscayans themselves, and ships of several more countries and free ports, were to be seen heading northwards as soon as winter had passed. In England the 'Company for the Discovery of Unknown Countries', more commonly known as the Muscovy Company, which had been founded during the reign of Queen Elizabeth I to promote trade between England and Russia, considered that they held exclusive right to this new source of wealth—and were prepared to use force to support their claim.

Tempers flared. The ships of the Muscovy Company armed to drive off any interlopers found themselves outnumbered and out-gunned by the great Dutch whaling fleets which, by 1620, had started to move north. Faced with this show of force the English gave way and an uneasy peace settled on the Arctic seas. As firstcomers the English stayed in the bays on the south of Spitsbergen, the Dutch for the most part operated around Jan Mayen Island, 500 miles to the south-west. The Spaniards and the French worked the northern side of Spitsbergen.

There was no cause for conflict, there were whales and enough for everyone. The ships would anchor and remain at anchor in the bays while the whaleboats, as 'flimsy as a bubble' would catch their whales always within sight of the parent ships. By the middle of the seventeenth century, upwards of 300 vessels from half a dozen and more nations would make for Spitsbergen, Jan Mayen and Bear Islands, by far the greater proportion Dutch.

Every year an exodus took place from the Dutch home ports. The destination of these little ships, double-crewed for the occasion, was

The sperm whale was a ferocious quarry to be treated with awe and respect.

usually the summer village of Smeerenburg on Jan Mayen Island. Here communities were set up—numbering nearly 10,000 people or more on shore alone. There were traders and shopkeepers, workers for the whale-oil 'factories' established ashore in permanent buildings, and others making the best of this lucrative new industry. There were even bakers—when fresh loaves were ready a horn was sounded. The season was a short one of only three months, but it was a highly profitable business and for 130 years the Dutch remained dominant in these and other Arctic waters. The English interest was variable but slight; that of the free ports of Hamburg and Bremen fairly constant and successful. Other nations also participated in the bonanza which directly or indirectly employed nearly 100,000 people in western Europe, gathering, processing or handling whale products.

Occasional attempts were made to overwinter on the barren shores of Spitsbergen or Jan Mayen Island. The Dutch efforts ended in disaster, and those of the English were just as unsuccessful. Even when criminals were promised their lives, many chose death rather than risk the unknown terrors of an Arctic winter. After a lot of difficulty the Muscovy Company at last persuaded a small party to agree, but when they saw the bleakness of the place they rescinded and were brought home. Whether the magistrates were impressed by the good sense shown by the criminal classes on this occasion, or if the intercession of the captain on their behalf swayed the day, these intrepid men were pardoned, and Spitsbergen continued to be abandoned every autumn. A party of shipwrecked English sailors did survive in these terrible regions, existing over one winter on whale remains, but they were considered to have borne charmed lives and no further serious attempts were made to occupy the whaling stations during the winter months.

The quarry of the hunters was the Greenland right whale (known on both sides of North America to a later generation as the bowhead) which frequents Arctic waters. Sixty-foot long with whalebone which can reach 14 foot, like its relative the black right, this great creature is a member of the baleen family, which are distinguished by being toothless (unlike the other whale family, the toothed whales, of which the sperm is the best-known member). Instead of teeth the baleens are furnished with whalebone—long horny plates hanging down from the upper jaw and each little more than half an inch thick, firm on the outside but on the inside of the mouth covered with thick bristles. It is through these bristles that the whale sucks its food—enormous quantities of a small shrimp-like creature, the krill, which live in icy waters. The baleen whale has a double blowhole—whereas the toothed whales have only one. But like all whales, they produce their young alive in water—differing from most mammals, though, these young make their entry into the world tail first.

But to the early whale hunters, a whale was a whale. A massive creature yielding astonishing quantities of oil which could be used for lighting and heating, as a lubricant and a base for paint, soap and the processing of jute. The 'whalebone', or baleen, was of even greater value. At one time it even reached the astonishing price of £2,500 a ton. At that rate the products from a single whale were more than enough to pay for the cost of a voyage to the Arctic.

Baleen or whalebone.

Whalebone was used for many purposes which are today served by steel or plastic. It was highly malleable and when heated could be shaped at will, and then held its shape; it was extremely strong, and could be cut easily. It was widely used as bones for corsets or stays and in umbrellas or parasols. When cut in finer strips it could serve in place of wicker, and when finer still, for sieves, nets and brushes. If brought back as blubber rather than oil, the remains, the 'finks', were excellent as manure. Many nations prized whale meat highly, while the ground-up bones served several purposes.

Early hunting methods were simple—and hardly altered over 300 years. The flimsy whaleboats with whalemen using hand-held harpoons attached to lengths of cable—as much as a quarter of a mile, neatly coiled in barrels amidships—would set out as soon as a whale was sighted. As an English captain described it:

The whalers sought their quarry in every ocean. Whalers off the Cape of Good Hope.

They row as fast as they possibly can after the whale, but must be very cautious they don't come too near his tail; when they come pretty near him, they are silent and make as little noise with the oars as they possibly can. When they are near enough the Harpuneer throws his harpun with all his force; this harpun is about three feet long, having on both sides hooks or notches to prevent its being torn out again . . . The whale with incredible swiftness goes towards the bottom of the sea; so that the line smoaks, being rubbed against the sides of the chalop (or whaleboat), and would certainly take fire if the men did not continually pour water upon it . . . When they find him almost tired and his strength considerable abated, they draw nearer to him and make use of other lances which resemble our pikes till they have hit his lungs or liver, at which the fish spouts out a vast quantity of blood through the pipes which rises into the air as high as the mast. The fish begins to rage most furiously till the sea is all in a foam and when he strikes his tail at the waves you may hear it half a league distance. Having lost all his strength he turns upon one side, and as soon as he is dead upon his back; then they draw him with ropes either ashore (if it be near Spitsbergen) or else to the ship.

The final flurry. Sperm whale fishing in the Atlantic.

Dragged ashore by huge capstans, the carcases were cut in pieces. The blubber, which could be over one foot thick in the Greenland right whale, was cut into convenient sizes and placed in coppers to boil, the resulting oil cooled and then ladled into barrels. The great heads, which in right whales comprise a third of the total length, were hoisted on a mast, the whalebone cut out and trimmed to convenient lengths, the rest of the head also boiled for its oil. If too far off-shore for the carcase to be handled in this way, the dead whale was lashed head and tail to the side of the vessel and then using sharp 'spades' a length of blubber was cut, a hole made in the end through which a rope was fastened and then the blubber peeled off in spiral fashion, cut in chunks and stored in casks.

By 1750 even the seemingly inexhaustible whale stocks around Spitsbergen and other Arctic islands were hunted out. The whales had quitted the bays and moved to the banks—the underwater mountains lying beyond the islands, and when driven from there had retired to the great ice fields to the north and west. The huge seal herds in waters west of Greenland were already attracting hunters from a dozen nations, now the whalers joined in and combined sealing with whaling. Seals were taken in the early part of the season, and whales—including the small Arctic bottlenose—when the pack ice had melted to allow the ships into the whale-rich northern Arctic waters. Spitsbergen and Smeerenburg were abandoned. The other summer whaling settlements sank into decline and, battered by wind and Arctic weather, the shore factories crumbled into ruin.

Now the whalers were faced with a different type of hunting. This was no longer a task for the small flimsy craft which had made the annual passage to Spitsbergen and Jan Mayen Island. In the uncompromising waters around Baffin Island and in the Davis Strait west of Greenland, stronger and larger boats were needed to battle with pack ice and Arctic conditions. Harried by the hunters, the whales retreated further and further north and were pursued into the deepest recesses of Arctic waters by determined skippers. Now ships of another nation joined those from Europe in the systematic destruction of the Arctic stocks.

The seamen of the American colonies were late on the scene. Sure enough 'drift' whales, as they were called, were cast up on the shores of New England and Long Island, and in considerable numbers. Later, small boats would venture out into the 'deep', take the single whale which was the limit of their capacity and return. The whales they took were the black right, the gray whale—which was then to be found on the eastern side of North America (although it is now solely associated with the Pacific)—and the humpback. Becoming more adventurous, the New Englanders began to sail further afield. So it came about that in 1712 a whaling boat was blown far into the Atlantic and came across a sperm whale.

This was a wholly different kind of whale to the other kinds they had

Illustrations (on this page and right) from Greasy Luck—A Whaling Sketchbook *by Gordon Grant.*

been taking previously. The sperm was of about the same size as the right whale—some 60 feet in length—but there the similarities seemed to end. Instead of the great bow-shaped jaws of the right whale with its latticework of baleen, the sperm whale had an enormous gape, fitted with a formidable row of lower teeth—the upper ones hidden under layers of gum. Like the right whale, the head of the creature occupied a third of its total length, but the forepart contained an enormous tank or reservoir holding gallon after gallon of a clear substance which hardened to wax when exposed to the air. This was the spermaceti, the most valuable of whale oils, and when mixed with the oil from rendered-down sperm whale blubber was marketed as sperm oil—nowadays the spermaceti is kept separate and is used for special ointments. (A sperm oil substitute has now been found in the seeds of the jojoba plant, a desert shrub, so the sperm whale may soon lose a good deal of its commercial importance.)

Soon American whale ships were venturing north to join the European fleets in the Arctic. There they hunted the survivors of the Greenland right whale, seal and polar bears, while other Yankee skippers roamed the Atlantic searching for the great sperm whale herds. The centre of this thriving industry was New England—in 1771 the State of Massachusetts alone furnished over 300 whale-hunting vessels which ranged the Atlantic Ocean from Iceland to the tropics, from the 'Brazil banks' to the coast of Africa. A usual port of call was the Cape Verde Islands off the west coast of Africa, and most New England whaling crews numbered a few Cape Verdeans—for Cape Verde then had a powerful reputation as a home of tough boatmen and harpooners who had been brought up from infancy to hunt the whale. They used techniques which to this day are practised in the Azores and latterly in Madeira.

On these long voyages often in tropical heat, fermenting blubber steaming in wooded casks was enough to upset the strongest stomachs, and did no good to the quality of the resulting whale oil, so instead, open fires in brick grates were built on deck and in these 'try works', as they were called, the blubber was boiled and the oil collected. Although a hazardous business, few ships were burned, and the advantages of the practice far outweighed the potential risk of fire or the other inherent and manifold perils of whaling.

To the whalers, the right whale, either Greenland or black, had proved a placid, almost docile creature, but the sperm was a very different quarry and whaling men treated him with respect and awe. 'There are two sorts of whales' they would say, 'One of 'em is the sperm whale; the rest of 'em is the other.' Armed with a formidable lower jaw and an enormous mouth the sperm whale was also a natural fighter. Often he would vent his wrath on the flimsy whaleboats, occasionally turning on the parent ship with devastating results. His technique was to roll on his back and snap at anything and everything in his path with his huge jaws. Sometimes this antic would be preceeded by an action called 'pitch-poling' by the whalemen, when the whale would, as it were, stand on his tail and bobbing up and down slowly revolve viewing its assailants. If the jaw was frightening enough, the tail held even greater terrors. 'In the tail,' wrote William Scoresby, one of the great early whaling writers, 'lays the whole strength of the whale, it is the fisherman's greatest fear, the power and the weight so great that boats are stove, upset, perhaps completely severed in two, sometimes thrown quite out of the water, or crushed to atoms beneath the stroke.'

The perils of whaling were considerable even before the taking of sperm whales, but the sperm added a new dimension. A skipper wrote of the battle of flimsy boats against the leviathan of the deep:

> We lowered two boats for a full sperm whale. The nearest boat met him head on, and, when abreast of the hump, the boat steerer put two irons into him. Before the boat could be brought head on, the whale broached half out of the water and capsized her, the line fouling the boat steerer's leg, almost severing it from the body. With great presence of mind he cut the line, and the other boat picked up the upset crew and returned to the bark. But the whale was not satisfied with his victory over the boat . . . making for the bark he struck her an tremendous blow . . . A second time he struck the vessel but with much less force.

At length after more hair-raising adventures the whale was secured. It produced 103 barrels of oil, 'the reward of its capture'. No wonder the whalers' motto, 'A dead whale or a stove boat' had such a depth of meaning to those who ventured after the whale.

Under the increasing weight of international hunting, the then known whale populations of the world dwindled almost visibly. No longer could the whale boats venture into Greenland waters and be guaranteed a worthwhile catch. Catastrophe had befallen a number of fleets over the years, now owners were reluctant to replace their lost craft when the hope of profit was so slim. By the end of the eighteenth century the Greenland whale fisheries were in serious decline, and the sperm whale herds were becoming increasingly hard to locate. Other grounds were needed.

In 1787 a British whale ship, the *Emilia*, manned by Nantucket whalemen, who had quitted America during the War of Independence, had passed round Cape Horn and come across seemingly limitless stocks of the southern strain of the black right whale off the western coast of South America. The good news soon travelled. Four years later six ships from Nantucket and New Bedford made the same dangerous passage and found the same immense stocks of whales. Soon the South Pacific fisheries reached an importance as great as that of the Greenland waters of old. And like the Greenland waters, the South Pacific was soon almost devoid of whales.

In 1836 a number of whaling boats cruising off the coast of Chile had wearied of finding so few whales and left, journeying north. They found whales all right—the Pacific strain of the Greenland right whale, the bowhead, and they also found such unseasonable weather of dense fog, and pack ice that they declared these northern waters unfishable. Necessity proved them wrong, however, and by the middle of the nineteenth century larger and larger fleets of whaling ships were hunting on the north-west grounds of the Pacific. The heyday of the great Alaskan fisheries was dawning.

Elsewhere, by the first decades of the nineteenth century, the oceans of the world were being traversed by the whaling ships of many nations. At first it was off the coast of Africa, then in the Indian Ocean off Zanzibar, and in the western Pacific. As each new hunting ground was found, it was hunted to exhaustion and then the whalers went off anew.

A favourite voyage of the 1840s was to touch the Azores, follow down the west coast of Africa, and rounding the Cape of Good Hope, cross the Indian Ocean to Australia and the South Pacific. Whalers then might turn north to Japan or the Bering Strait, or else hunt the 'offshore' Pacific grounds. And voyages lasted for several years, with the ships passing their load of oil or whalebone to empty cargo ships to carry home. The quarry was the bowhead, humpback or gray whale in the Japanese seas, the humpback or the ubiquitous sperm whale in Australian or New Zealand waters. The Galapagos Islands was a regular port of call. Here under a huge whitened and weathered turtle shell was the whalemen's post-office and every ship on its way out or back called in to deliver or pick up mail.

It was a strange life, living in a whaleship at sea for three years or more—the record was for a voyage of 11 years by the *Nile* from New London. The risks of death through injury or sickness were high, and every ship assumed a high rate of desertion when they called at the South Sea Islands. But they always managed to make up strength from those who had deserted from previous whale ships and desertion was an accepted way of life. When challenged by a churchman on one of the South Sea Islands a whale skipper was said to have replied, 'Brother, if I cleared my ship for Heaven tomorrow, and touched at Hell next month, ev'ry damn one of 'em would desert if he got a chance!' It was little the wonder that the much shorter six month Arctic voyage of the New England whale boats in the Atlantic were scathingly referred to as 'plum pudding' trips.

The catching techniques were much as practised before, but now hand-held harpoons had been succeeded in many cases by harpoon guns mounted in the prow of the whaleboats. An innovation first tried in 1730—but then abandoned as being more dangerous to the firer than any passing whale—and then reintroduced 50 years later to a new design. The old lance too had been replaced by one with an explosive head, so that the process of killing was much accelerated.

Hand-held harpoons were succeeded by harpoon guns. A contemporary print of the 1870s.

By the middle of the nineteenth century the centre of American whaling had shifted from New England to the Pacific ports, and principally San Francisco and Honolulu. The American North Pacific fleet primarily operated in Japanese and Alaskan waters. As they waited for the ice to break, they would sail south for the sperms, and then head north for the bowheads and although less dangerous than the sperm whale the bowhead lived in waters where ice was an ever-present hazard. In 1871 of a whale fleet of 40 ships, only seven survived, the rest were caught and then crushed in the ice floes.

Increasingly, as stocks became scarce, a number of skippers chose to over-winter on the bleak shores of north Canada and Alaska. When the ice melted in the spring they were ready to take the best of what was rapidly becoming a sparse crop.

To add to the problems of whaling economics, whale oil was now challenged by petroleum oils and, as a result, the price plumetted. Whalebone was still in demand, but here too alternatives such as steel were making inroads into what had previously been the exclusive province of baleen. It was still commercially worthwhile to send ships to the whaling regions of the North Pacific, but more whales were now needed to make an economic cargo, and it was becoming very apparent that the vast whale stocks of old were no longer there. A number of skippers had already voiced concern over the huge quantities of whales taken each year and the effect it was having on stocks. It had been calculated that a fleet of 300 whaling vessels in the North Pacific, as in the 1840s, were killing annually the equivalent of 18,000 whales—within ten years the whaling fleets in the North Pacific were nearing 800 sail. In 1852 a whaling skipper wrote that the whale, chased from sea to sea, and from haunt to haunt, 'is doomed to utter extermination, or so near it, that few will remain to tempt the cupidity of man.' This gloomy augury looked like being fulfilled, and sooner than anyone had expected. By the 1860s a number of ships were returning from Alaskan waters with two, perhaps three whales to show for a full season's activities. Even the gray whale which had once frequented the Californian lagoons had been fished to the point of extermination.

During the early years of whaling prosperity the whale fleets of many nations had suffered crippling, sometimes irreplacable losses. The Civil War of 1860 saw serious inroads into the American east coast fleet and earlier the British whaling fleet in the North Atlantic had been dealt a crippling blow with 54 vessels crushed by ice, although, astonishingly, not a man was lost. Now economic circumstances seemed about to sound the death knell to the industry. In the years following the American Civil War the whaling fleets started to show a swift and steady decline. The San Francisco squadron began to disappear and the whaling industry which had employed so many, either directly or indirectly appeared to be doomed. Thus by the early 1860s the great whale stocks of the North Atlantic were no more. Those in the South Pacific were seriously depleted, to the extent that they were no longer worth hunting, while those which had once seemed inexhaustible in the North Pacific were all but wiped out. Meanwhile the sperm whales which were to be found in every ocean of the world were being harried by whalers of a dozen nations. Even so, it is probable that the several species of whale then surviving would have continued to do so without threat of extinction despite the slaughter at the hands of the whaling skippers, had it not been for a radical shift in technology—the explosive-headed harpoon.

The inventor of the device which was to revolutionize whale fishing and to prove the single most decisive threat to the survival of the whale

'Cutting in' a sperm whale. The blubber was peeled off the dead whale in spiral fashion.

as a species was a Norwegian, Svend Foyn. Foyn was a highly experienced seaman and seal master and, ironically, he was described in later life as 'a most fortunate, religious and good old man, respected and beloved by all who met him.' He little knew what he had done.

From time to time when hunting northern or deep southern waters, skippers had harpooned another type of whale, one vastly bigger and stronger than any other, usually with calamitous results. This was truly the leviathan of legend. Tales abounded of its great size and strength. One whaleboat managed to harpoon one of these monsters only to see its line run off in a matter of seconds. The crew managed to hitch on to another boat, and another, and finally on to the whaleship itself and this quaint procession of three whaleboats and the parent ship was towed for 14 hours until finally wearying of the unequal chase the whaleship's engine was put into reverse and the line was snapped. On rare occasions, though, specimens of these great whales had been taken, and then it was discovered that when they died they sank quickly. Indeed the story was recited of a whale ship which after days and weeks of fruitless hunting at last slew a whale. They hauled it alongside, but so overjoyed were they that they set to celebrating the great occasion without carrying out the elementary precaution of first making the whale fast. When the carousing came to an end and they were ready to set about the grisly task of cutting up the great creature, the whale was no longer there—it had sunk without trace.

These leviathans which had so amazed and alarmed the whalers were blue whales. A colossal creature of up to 100 feet in length and weighing up to 150 tons—equivalent to 25 elephants or 1,600 human beings. It roamed the oceans of the world from the Arctic to the Antarctic, from the vastness of the Pacific to the Roaring Forties in the Indian Ocean.

The blue whale is a member of a family of baleen whales known as the rorquals (a name derived from the Norwegian *rörhval*, which refers to the deep grooves which run on the underside from the lower lip to the centre of the body). The rorquals are more streamlined and their baleen much shorter than that of the right whales. The principal rorquals are the blue, fin and humpback, each of which, in turn, have been fished to the verge of extinction, and all will sink when dead, thus they were largely immune from the depredations of the whalers until the arrival of Foyn's invention.

Foyn mounted his gun with his new harpoon in the bows of the ironically named *Spes et Fides* (Hope and Faith), a small 90 foot steamer of 86 tons, with a top speed of seven knots. To counteract the dead weight of a sunken whale she was equipped with a powerful winch, and to cushion the shock of a dead whale dangling below the ship in a heavy sea, an 'accumulator' of heavy springs was mounted in the rigging, while to stop the dead whale sinking it became the custom to pump steam or compressed air into the carcase.

The combination of steam power and the explosive-headed harpoon heralded a new and more lethal age of whale hunting.

The lethal harpoon was equipped with moveable barbs which opened like the flukes of a folding anchor when pulled away, and as they opened they set off an explosive charge designed to kill instantaneously. Thus the Foyn harpoon combined harpoon and the old explosive-headed lance, and with it the task of killing whales took a new turn. What had once been laborious and highly dangerous now became almost simple, and with the advent of the steam-powered catcher, ruthlessly efficient. In 1868 the *Spes et Fides* made her inaugural voyage, and took an almost unprecedented 30 whales. The fate of the rorqual whales was sealed.

By the turn of this present century, the whaling industry, which had once seemed in serious decline due to reduction in whale stocks, had revived. The Norwegians were in the lead. Their own waters were yielding over 1,000 whales a year, and as these stocks diminished so they cast further afield establishing whaling stations in Iceland, the Faroes, in Labrador, Newfoundland, Africa, South America, Australia and even on the coast of Spain. Other nations were quick to adopt the new method and to set up their own whaling stations. The Russians in the North Atlantic and North Pacific. The French in Madagascar and on the West African coast in Gabon. The great whale hunt was on. Now no whale was immune, no species too fast nor too strong for the whalers' equipment.

The first decade of the twentieth century saw the apogee of whaling effort and a marked decline in the stock of the larger whales. But the new method of whale catching had made it possible for the whalers to crop the great southern and Antarctic seas for the first time. Here, as at Spitsbergen, and on Jan Mayen and Bear Islands, nearly two centuries before, whale factories were set up on shore. The first was in South Georgia in 1905. Six years later there was a total of ten on the Antarctic mainland and a further 14 factory ships moored in the great bays of the Antarctic continent. At first these factory ships remained at anchor, but then they started to accompany their flotilla of smaller whale catchers as the latter scoured the southern seas.

The First World War marked the virtual end of the old wooden whaling ships. The next great advance in whale-hunting technique came in 1925 with the introduction of factory ships with stern slipways, up which carcases could be dragged. But could whale stocks survive such an onslaught? In the 1930/31 season, an incredible 43,000 whales were taken, of which 29,000 were blues.

In 1935 the first efforts at international cooperation under the auspices of the League of Nations took place. Two years later the British, Norwegian, German governments and those of other whaling nations agreed to impose size limits on the blue whales, as well as banning completely the taking of gray and right whales.

The Second World War provided something of a breathing space for the populations of the larger whales and in 1946 the International Whaling Commission was formed to regulate and control worldwide

Spitsbergen, 1905.

Blue whale slaughter in the Antarctic.

whalehunting. The truest indictment, though, of man's depredation on the whale stocks of the world lies in the grim catalogue of banned species: in 1955 hunting for the humpback whale was banned in the North Atlantic, and in 1966 it was made a wholly protected species. This was the same year that hunting for the blue whale was forbidden in the southern hemisphere and the following year it too became wholly protected. The fin whale was totally protected except for small catches in restricted areas in 1975. And now the sei whale, in 1979, is also totally protected in the southern hemisphere. On the other side of the coin, the gray whale, protected in 1937 and with a then estimated worldwide population of no more than 250 adults, has recovered to the extent that a limited quota is once more permitted.

Just as the old whalers exploited each area in turn, so modern whaling is a catalogue of the exploitation of whale species in turn. As the stock of the blue whale declined, so the fin whale took its place. When around 1962 the fin started to become scarce, so it was the turn of the sei whale. The majority of whales taken now are sperm whales and it is clear that the average size and weight of those killed has been reducing significantly, a sure indication of over-hunting. The permitted sperm whale take has steadily reduced; in the season 1975/6 it was 19,000, in 1976/7, 11,999; in 1977/8 no more than 4,635 and at the latest meeting of the 18 members of the International Whaling Commission the quota has been reduced still further.

At the same meeting Russia announced that it would end commercial whaling over the next five years and there is an increasingly powerful lobby for declaring a moratorium on the taking of all whales, a proposal stoutly opposed by the Japanese who still eat considerable quantities of whale meat. All whaling in the Indian Ocean has now been banned, but the words of the whalers' sea shanty ring ironically:

> O, the whale is free, of the boundless sea;
> He lives for a thousand years;
> He sinks to rest on the billow's breast,
> Nor the roughest tempest fears.
> The howling blast, as it rushes past,
> Is music to lull him to sleep.

Some Whales of the World

Blue Whale
Killer Whale
Greenland Right Whale
Narwhal
Fin Back Whale
Pilot Whale
Sperm Whale
Beluga Whale
Humpback Whale

2 Fur Fever

Friend, once 'twas Fame that led thee forth
To brave the Tropick Heat, the Frozen North,
Late it was Gold, then Beauty was the Spur;
But now our Gallants venture but for fur.

    *Dryden, on the occasion of the first Auction
    of the Hudson's Bay Company, London, 1671.*

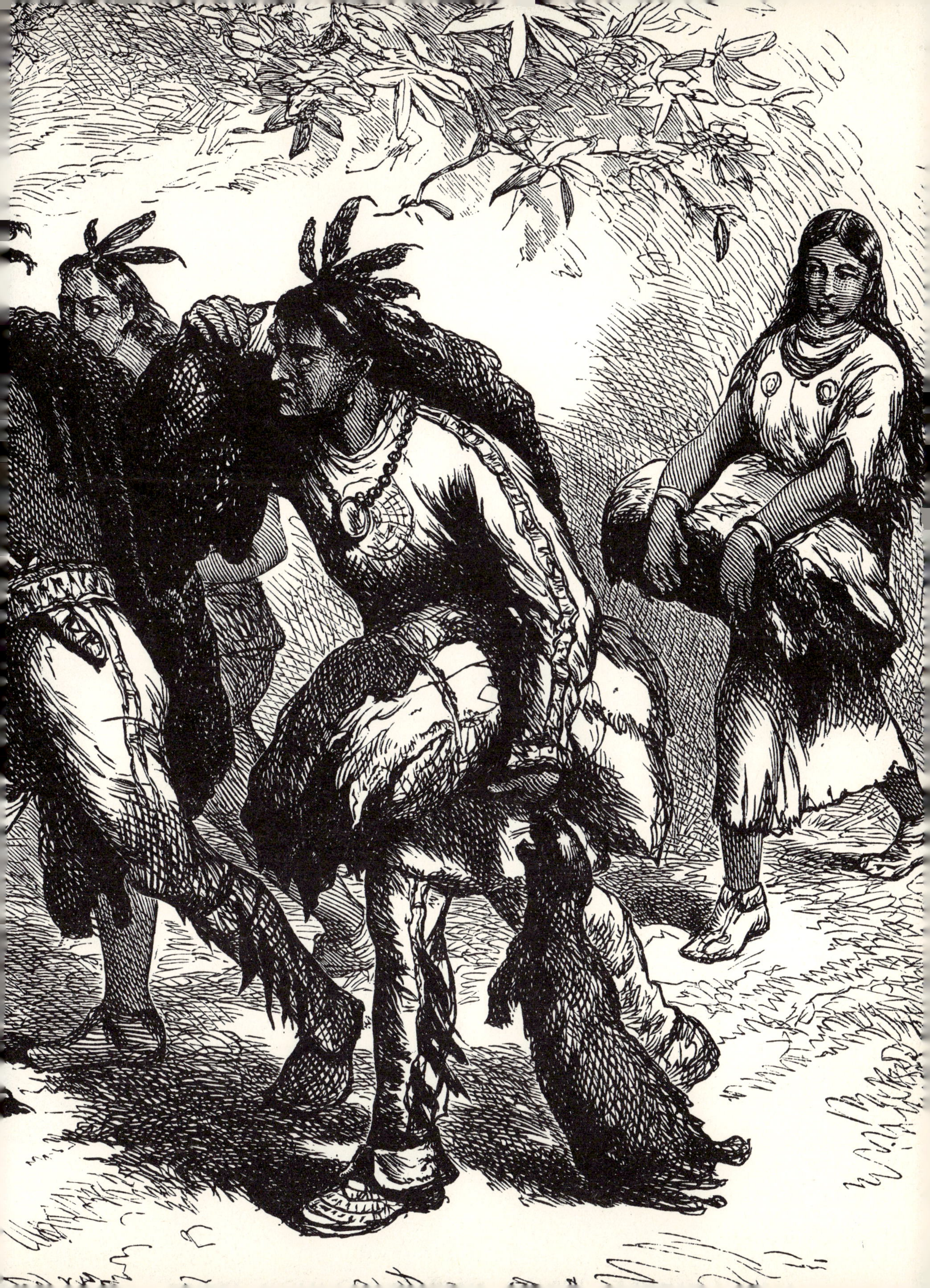

For man from earliest times furs have been a necessity, a luxury, the currency of ransom, the stuff of trade, the gifts of monarchs, the distinguishing mark of rank and fashion. In 2182 BC Queen Semiramis of Egypt brought back 800 tiger skins as tribute from India. In Homer's time there was a thriving fur trade with Siberia, Russia, Persia and Bokhara—its centre Byzantium. The early Church Fathers in Rome condemned the use of furs as a barbaric luxury. Marco Polo on his great Asian adventures comments on the magnificent furs worn by the rulers of Tartary and the ermines and sables which lined their tents. Returning crusaders brought back costly furs from their wars.

The extensive forests which covered most of the Medieval landscape of Europe were full of fur-bearing animals. The rivers held beaver and otter, while deer, lynx, wolf and fox were common in the forests. The European beaver had a range which extended from the shores of the Mediterranean—where it was called the Pontic dog—to Scandinavia; from the Atlantic to the depths of Russia and Siberia. The lynx was found in much of France and was a menace in Spain. In 1419 a wolf was seen in the very streets of Paris.

In Britain, where the beaver was still found extensively, and wolves were not uncommon, of the animals known today only the rabbit was virtually unknown. Originally imported from the continent, it was still confined to the islands of the Bristol Channel and the sandy coastal regions of the mainland. Further inland, fox and wolf held sway, for not until the thirteenth century did the rabbit start to seriously spread inland; but within 200 years so successful and promiscuous had it become that a considerable export trade in coney skins was being carried on with the continent.

The rarer and more beautiful skins were hunted assiduously. An eleventh-century geographer wrote, 'for our damnation, as I believe... we strive as hard to come into the possession of a marten skin as if it were everlasting salvation.' For as warmth and comfort were complemented by style and elegance, and man learned to make and weave cloth, furs became no longer a necessity but a luxury. The best furs were reserved for the rich and noble. Jealous of their prerogatives, the high in the land forbade lesser folk to wear those furs reserved for the cream of Medieval society. Ermine, sometimes referred to as white weasel or thought of as the fur of a white rat, has always been looked on as a regal fur; sable too was reserved for the privileged. Lesser mortals might wear the common squirrel, fox or sheepskins. Members of the Church were condemned to using the most wretched furs and only at their peril might the poor clothe themselves with fur above their position in life. It was an act of calculated humility to wear furs of a type lower than those entitled. Henry III of England would don sheepskins to the disgust and dismay of his courtiers who were constrained to follow his example. The Bishop of Worcester declined the beaver or sable to which his rank entitled him and, instead, chose lambskin. When challenged by his

Hunting in the far north. Three woodcuts from Olavus Magnus's Historia de Gentibus, *1555.*

A South American fur trapper.

priests and asked to at least wear catskins as more befitting his station, he is said to have replied, 'Believe me, men oftener sing of the Lamb of God, than of the Cat of God!'

It was easier, however, to make such ordinances than to keep them and a merchant was heard to exclaim that it was hard to tell apart 'a tapester, a cookesse, or a Hosteller's wife from a Gentilwoman.'

The demand for furs in Europe in the Middle Ages was prodigious. A robe for Henry IV of England required no less than 12,000 squirrel and 80 ermine skins. The order from the English court alone in a single year was for 80,000 furs 'of the better sort'. But this was nothing compared to the 250,000 ermines needed for the sumptuous coronation robes of an early czar.

The forests, however, where the fur animals were to be found, were fast disappearing. Indiscriminate cutting and burning of timber, was carried on with no control and little hindrance. Church and state showed considerable concern at this loss of woodland and in many countries preservation orders were imposed. Not only did the forest provide timber for shipbuilding, but it also fuelled iron smelting and other industries. The preserved forests were looked on as game reserves for hunting by crown, church and the nobility, and many of today's fine forests in parts of Germany and eastern Europe owe their survival to this patronage.

Nevertheless, by the sixteenth century great stretches of Germany had been wholly denuded, tracts of Poland, Hungary, Bohemia and elsewhere stripped of woods. In Castile in Spain, not only had the forests been cleared but the surviving woodlands opened to the ravages of sheep, the efforts of which were aided by wanton burning of scrub to create even more grazing land, ultimately leading to severe erosion.

As forests all over Europe were pushed back to make way for agricultural land, the habitat of many indigenous animals began to shrink. The timid marten, so beloved of medieval furriers was soon confined to only the most inaccessible parts of the wilder retreats. In Scotland, indeed, the export of marten skins was prohibited altogether in the eleventh century due to the 'exhorbitant dearth' of the animal. By 1200, in Britain, the beaver was only to be found on the River Teifi in Wales and on the River Dee and one or two other places in Scotland. Elsewhere in Europe its range was becoming more and more restricted.

The European beaver, which differs only slightly from its North American relation, was at a peculiar disadvantage. Its skin was covetted by those in the West, while to seal its fate the supposed medicinal virtues of the musk glands were desired especially in the East where the castorium they produced was a cure-all for every disease or ailment from deafness, to pleurisy, apoplexy, hiccoughs and weakened sight. For rheumatism it was considered a sovereign remedy, for surely, it was thought, the beaver's own watery existence must give immunity. For epilepsy there was nothing so effective as sleeping on a beaver pelt.

An excellent tonic was ground-up beaver teeth in soup. And if that was not enough to condemn the creature to annihilation, the musk gland secretion was used as the base for many flower scents, and its tail was considered a delicacy fit for the greatest tables. By 1526 the last British beaver is believed to have vanished, by 1600 it was even becoming scarce in Scandinavia, although still numerous further east. Soon indiscriminate hunting had eliminated it altogether from southern and much of central Europe and this, despite the creation of beaver reserves in Germany and a number of other countries.

Beyond the forest boundaries the increasing volume of domestic stock was especially vulnerable to predator attack, and in their own interest peasants slaughtered any predator they could find. Wolves, once commonplace in France, were hounded to near extinction and by the seventeenth century were to be found only in the most inaccessible parts of the country; an elimination which was to have almost immediate effect on the quality of the deer herds—an experience echoed on several occasions, with caribou in Canada and reindeer in Norway.

With western Europe becoming fast hunted out, it was fortunate that a comparatively untouched source lay at hand.

It had long been known that the best furs were to be obtained from the colder northern regions. And there were none better than those from Russia and Scandinavia which were of a beauty, depth of colour, lustre and quality which could not be challenged by furs from further south. Since the ninth century a thriving commerce had been carried on along one of the oldest trade routes in the world—that from the Baltic to Constantinople and the Near East. And it was to the East that the European fur traders turned once western European supplies were nearing exhaustion.

Up and down the ancient trade route would travel caravans making use of the network of rivers in summer, or by sledge in winter. With wine, fruits, cloth and fine textiles, occasionally gold, silver or silk from the markets of the Near East they also carried the fur riches of northern Europe—the dark sable of incredible softness and lustre, the marten fit for the robes of the highest, delicate white fur of the ermine, squirrel pelts by the hundred thousand, the beaver and the otter.

Through the fourteenth and fifteenth centuries a non-stop supply of all kinds and in prodigious quantities came from the apparently limitless stocks of Russia, from the plains, forests and vast expanse of the land to the east. Here was a wealth of pelts of all sorts and of the best varieties. The red squirrel was found in such remarkable abundance that it was popularly supposed to be carried in the clouds and to fall from heaven. Other squirrels from Scandinavia were of different colours. Those from the furthest north were of a distinctive blue-grey with a white belly; those from the forests of central Europe, black. In matching and blending lay the furrier's art, and when sewn together they made a highly attractive combination of alternating bands of light and dark colour, the whole known as *vair*. (Cinderella wore slippers of *vair* and not *verre* (glass) as has been mistranslated for centuries.)

As Russian expansion extended eastwards, so the great fur riches of Siberia came on the market and the tribes in what is now eastern Russia who for centuries had been passing their skins to markets in China, now found another outlet. This wholesale exploitation could have only one result. By the middle of the sixteenth century many parts of central and eastern Europe had been hunted out, and in addition there was a severe shortage of high class furs from the eastern part of Russia. No longer could the merchants of Novgorod, enjoy the fur wealth on their doorstep, now they were forced to send long and increasingly expensive hunting expeditions hundreds of miles into the hinterland in search of skins. There were still vast fur stocks in furthest Siberia, but these were also being systematically hunted out, and as the hunt moved ever eastwards it became increasingly expensive to supply a western market. Also fur was losing its appeal as a symbol of rank, and a number of countries actively supported their growing cloth industries at the expense of the skinners. There was also a gradual change in fashion as the wealthy increasingly spent extravagantly on velvets, brocades and fine fabrics.

Skin tanning in the sixteenth century.

As one who yearned for the old days complained, this was the age of 'silks, shagges and rags ...' Fine furs were in use too, but as embellishment—and an increasingly expensive one. Seldom now were full linings and facings seen, instead trimming with the better furs was practised. Also houses were warmer, there was less need to wear furs indoors. Even in Siberia, where once the natives had lined their snowshoes with sable, one observer reported that now they had to travel for over a month to find sables enough to hunt.

In Russia, Moscow had succeeded Novgorod as the great fur centre, and Novgorod itself was sacked by Ivan the Terrible in 1570. Seventeen years before, the voyage of the English explorer Richard Chancellor round the top of Norway, and North Cape to the White Sea had opened up the great fur wealth of north Russia which had been hardly touched and where were 'Fine furres as Sables, Martens ... Bevers, Foxes, Mixes, Ermines ... The North partes of Russia yield very rare and precious Skinnes.' The Muscovy Company, established for general trade in those parts, eagerly took up the new opportunity for commerce in furs, but only for a few years and soon reverted to their primary interest in providing naval stores for the expanding English navy—timber, wax, tallow and cordage. Everyone by then was finding furs too expensive, the better ones exhorbitantly so, for sable skins had 'growne to great excess, next unto gold and precious stones'.

This was partly due to the higher cost of transport, partly owing to severe political troubles in the Baltic states and Russia towards the end of the sixteenth century. However, the most important reason was the increasing scarcity of good pelts. Just as western Europe had turned to eastern Europe so now a new source presented itself.

That the North American continent possessed fabulous riches in furs was soon revealed to the early explorers. In 1524 Gomez, a Portuguese in the service of the King of Spain, in a journey that took him along the coasts of Nova Scotia and New England, returned to his royal master bringing with him some Indians 'who go covered with the skins of dyvers beasts both wylde and tame'. 'In their lands,' it was recorded, 'are many excellent furres as martens, sables, and such other rych furres, of which the sayde pilote Gomez brought summe with him into Spayne.' When the Basques, pursuing whales and walruses, landed in America they established a thriving sideline in fur trading with the Indians.

Later, Cabot set forth and crossed the great sea to seek for the fabled riches of Cathay. Instead of gold and 'all the spices of the world,' which he knew would be his, he found—cod. The fishermen who followed Cabot's great discovery soon found it more economical to gut and salt the fish on shore before turning for home. The metal knives they used proved a fascination to the Indian who had known only stone and bone implements, and it was not long before trade and barter with the local natives was under way. They traded for furs, and of these the beaver was the most beautiful, and the most numerous.

In the days when the first Europeans came to North America, abundant beaver colonies were to be found from the Gulf of Mexico in the south to the snow belt of the north, from the Atlantic to the Pacific. We must remember that, despite the often sentimentalized picture of the relationship between technological primitive man and those animals on which he relied, the beaver *did* live in harmony with the Red Indians of North America and assumed a special place in their lives—after all he provided nearly all their needs.

Beaver colonies were to be found a short distance from Indian villages, and Indian children would watch these remarkable builders constructing their dams: after all was it not said, 'consider the ways of the beaver and become wise'? When the Indians needed meat—and roast beaver was a great delicacy—or skins, although they preferred the skins of larger animals, they killed the wandering beaver leaving the colonies strictly alone—and thus practised a form of game management.

The bones were carefully collected and burned or thrown into the deepest part of the river or lake so that no dog or predator could defile the dead animal. For if they did so, the spirit of the beaver would be offended and cast a spell on their future hunting.

Beavers feature strongly in Indian folklore and legend. An Algonquin tribe from the area of Lake Huron, the Amikonas, saw themselves as the 'People of the Beaver', descendants of the great father of all beavers who had created the earth, and many other Indian tribes looked on the

A beaver lodge (from an eighteenth-century print).

beaver not as a quarry, but as their 'people'. Some legends had it that the animal was the reincarnation of men long dead and sent back to earth to atone for their sins. There were stories of intermarriage between beavers and women. Beaver robes often assumed almost mystical significance, frequently coupled with death. In some Indian legends a great beaver, Quahbeet, presided over the world. When he clapped his great broad tail on the ground the heavens thundered and the earth shook.

A beaver dam.

The Indian lived by hunting, and he hunted only to live. His weapons were the stone hatchet, the spear and the arrowhead. His methods were primitive but effective but he had not the means, if he had ever had the will, to hunt to extermination. He used the hides of the beasts he killed for tents and clothing and for shoes. When cut in long strips they made ropes and thongs. The furs he used for warmth and decoration. Of the bones he made arrowheads and needles. But the white man brought iron, and he later brought guns, and the 'civilising' process he also brought not only soon threatened and sometimes extinguished the animal life he found, it also undermined the inherent morality of the American Indian—as it was later to do to the African native. The killing of beaver as occasion demanded was succeeded by greed. For the Indian, now offered riches beyond his dreams and caught in the toils of the fur trade, set about slaughtering on a grand scale. The process was to change the face of a continent and a way of life centuries old.

'The Beaver is the bigness of a water-spaniel. Its fur is chestnut, black and rarely white and always very soft and suitable for the making of hats,' wrote an early observer of the extraordinary animal. At one time the wearing of beaverskin waistcoats was in vogue in Paris, and beaver leather was often used for making shoes. But from 1650 to 1820 it was for hats that the beaver pelt was needed. Not just for the well-to-do, although it was they who wore the finest, but for ordinary people as an increasing prosperity spread in Europe. The beaver skin combined warmth with quite remarkable softness, and for the feltmakers the smooth underfur with fine barbs at the end of each hair, which made them stick to the felt, was the ideal medium for their skills. At first the two-inch guard hairs had to be removed. In the best skins this had already been done by the Indians themselves who in wearing the pelts had worn away the outer hairs to expose the soft inner ones, no more than one inch long so desired by the hatmakers—and it was these worn skins that commanded the best prices.

The systematic slaughter of the beaver began in 1604 with the arrival of French trading posts on the St Lawrence River, which Jacques Cartier had discovered and followed upstream until he came upon a fine hill overlooking the broad river, which he called Mont Real. Cartier was succeeded by such men as Champlain, the explorer, and Pontgrave, the fur trader, and it was he who founded a trading post at a spot 'where the waters meet' and which the Indians called 'Ke-Bec'.

First French attempts to colonize the new land using convicts on the inhospitable Sable Island at the mouth of the St Lawrence ended with most of the 40 colonists being taken off by passing ships. Other attempts were little more successful and whereas in 1627 Virginia could boast a population of 4,000 colonists, there were no more than 100 living in the entire territory of New France. It was the reluctance of the French to capitalize on their explorations in North America, and therefore provide security for their fur traders, that accounted for their ultimate decline in the west. By the time they awoke to the fact that interlopers were threatening their preserves, the newcomers were too strong and too numerous to be ousted.

After the French had pressed westwards to the great lakes, the Dutch penetrated up the Hudson River and the Spaniards along the broad Mississippi, later colonists worked their way westwards over the Adirondacks. And as the European occupation of North America proceeded so the resident populations of beaver were pushed further and further back into the vast interior. Soon the once huge colonies in the east were finished and by 1635 the beaver had disappeared entirely from the Trois Rivières area of Canada downstream of Mont Real. At first the Indians had been careful to leave at least two beavers in each lodge, but greed became the better of them and soon there were only relics of beaver dams, falling to pieces and decaying in many parts of America.

The best fur-producing region of all was that around Hudson Bay. In 1668 at the suggestion of two French fur traders, Radisson and Groseilliers, who had abandoned the French service, a number of noble and distinguished gentlemen in London were persuaded to put up money for an expedition to gather furs in the area of Hudson Bay. Accordingly in that year two ships, the *Eaglet* and the *Nonsuch*, sailed from England bound for North America. The *Eaglet* was damaged en route and was forced to return, but the *Nonsuch* sailed on and reached James Bay at the southern end of Hudson Bay. Radisson and Groseilliers and the crew just had time to construct a building and a stockade which they called Fort Charles before winter clamped down.

Fur trading in North Canada (from a contemporary print).

When spring started to clear the ice, they began trading for furs with the local tribes and soon it became clear that around Hudson Bay was an area of fur riches beyond their wildest hopes. Groseilliers returned in triumph to England bringing a rich cargo of furs and buoyed by the success of the first trip, its sponsors sought a Royal Charter from King Charles II of England. On 2 May 1670, 'The Governor and Company of England Trading into Hudson's Bay' was duly established. This gave it the rights of 'sole trade and commerce within the entrance of Hudson Bay.' The first Governor of the new company was Prince Rupert, the King's cousin. So was created one of the greatest trading concerns the world has ever known. Under its generally benevolent eye a new continent was to be explored, and a new nation created.

For nearly 100 years a war of burned trading posts, captured furs and disputed territory smouldered between the French on the one hand and the interlopers from Hudson Bay. When not disputing with the French, the work of the Hudson's Bay Company went on. It was a lonely, isolated life in the trading posts along the shores of the bay and further into the interior of Canada as the fur trade moved westward. The waters of the Hudson Strait were free for navigation only from mid-July to the beginning of October each year so any outward or inward commerce had to be conducted during this narrow time span. Even then there was risk of fog, pack ice and ice floes, as well as the mischievous effect of the proximity of the magnetic pole which played havoc with the compass. They traded with the local Indians, the Crees

The first sale of furs by the Hudson's Bay Company at Garraway's Coffee House, London, 17 November 1671.

and Chipewyans, and the Assiniboines who gave up trading with the French in preference to doing business with the Hudson's Bay Company.

The Company would advance guns, powder, blankets, traps, meal and cloth, in exchange for only a promise—but that of a man who never broke his word.

In due time the trapper would return bearing with him his furs. Beaver for the most part, but also martens—the black marten was known as 'Hudson Bay sable'—otterskins, fox and muskrat pelts. Black beavers were the most highly priced and rare, brown beaver the staple. Occasionally ermine was brought in, silver fox and his rarer black cousin or even, very rarely, white fox, as well as mink, wolverine, skunk, lynx, wolf, red fox and bear. The brown beaver was not only the staple, it was also the unit of currency. Twelve beaverskins bought a gun, six a blanket, an axe cost three, a single pelt could buy ten ball-shot or half a pint of gunpowder.

An eighteenth-century fur shop.

Connoisseurs demanded Hudson's Bay furs which were known as the best on the continent and were nearly always taken at the height of winter when the pelt was at its most luxuriant. Other traders were not so fastidious and took pelts at all and every time of the year, thus even during the breeding season the fur-bearing animals were never left in peace. This effort at game management by the Hudson's Bay Company meant that the stocks of furs in their area lasted well beyond those elsewhere on the continent.

The monopoly of the Company was not to go unchallenged. In the

1790s a group of Montreal traders banded together to try to break the Hudson's Bay hold on the fur markets. This was the Northwest Company. Other rivals were also on the rise. The Southwest Company under the inspired hand of John Jacob Astor threatened the Canadian monopoly, especially when he formed his Pacific Fur Company and sought partnership with the Northwest. The principal battle, though, was between the two Canadian giants and by undercutting each other they threatened to bring both houses to financial ruin. In 1821 the two great companies united and law once more returned to the fur world of North America. The anarchy that had prevailed while the fur war had raged had stripped whole stretches of Canada of the beaver; now the Hudson's Bay rule of never killing in the breeding season, and the equally important one of never allowing liquor in the trading posts, permitted peace to return across much of the continent.

The great distances which now had to be covered to find the beaver and the cost of transporting pelts, raised their price dramatically. An increase in the number of trappers and better traps, principally metal ones, caused a further decline in fur stocks and this, in turn, meant a wider and wider search to make a living. As a result the production of furs in the first half of the last century declined by between one half and two thirds.

By the early 1800s the profitable range of beaver country lay north of the Great Lakes, except in the Rockies and the north-western states; elsewhere the beaver was to be found only in small and isolated communities. Voices were raised questioning how long the species could survive at the current rate of depredation for there seemed no sign at all of the demand for beaver skins slackening. Then once again, as has been the salvation of species on many occasions, the fickleness of fashion came to the rescue. Reprieve came in the discovery of apparently vast resources of a small fur-bearing animal, a native of the basin of the River Plate in South America, and of Brazil and Chile. This was the river rat or coypu whose colourful and fancy fur which was both plentiful and cheap appeared on the European market as nutria (from the Spanish *nutra*—otter). At nearly the same time and thanks to the machine age, fine textiles became cheaper than they had ever been before. Suddenly it was no longer fashionable to wear the 'beaver'; silk hats were the vogue.

By 1870 the price of beaver was a little more than one quarter of what it had been at the turn of the century, and although a surge of interest in the fur seal a few years later also revived trade in beaver skins and caused prices to rise, the huge demand responsible for the near extinction of the beaver never occurred again. Notwithstanding, nearly 3,000,000 beaver skins passed through the hands of the Hudson's Bay Company between the years 1853–77. The North American beaver had been saved, but it had been a very close thing.

If the demand for beaver skins was on the wane that for other furs

(Following pages) Trappers.

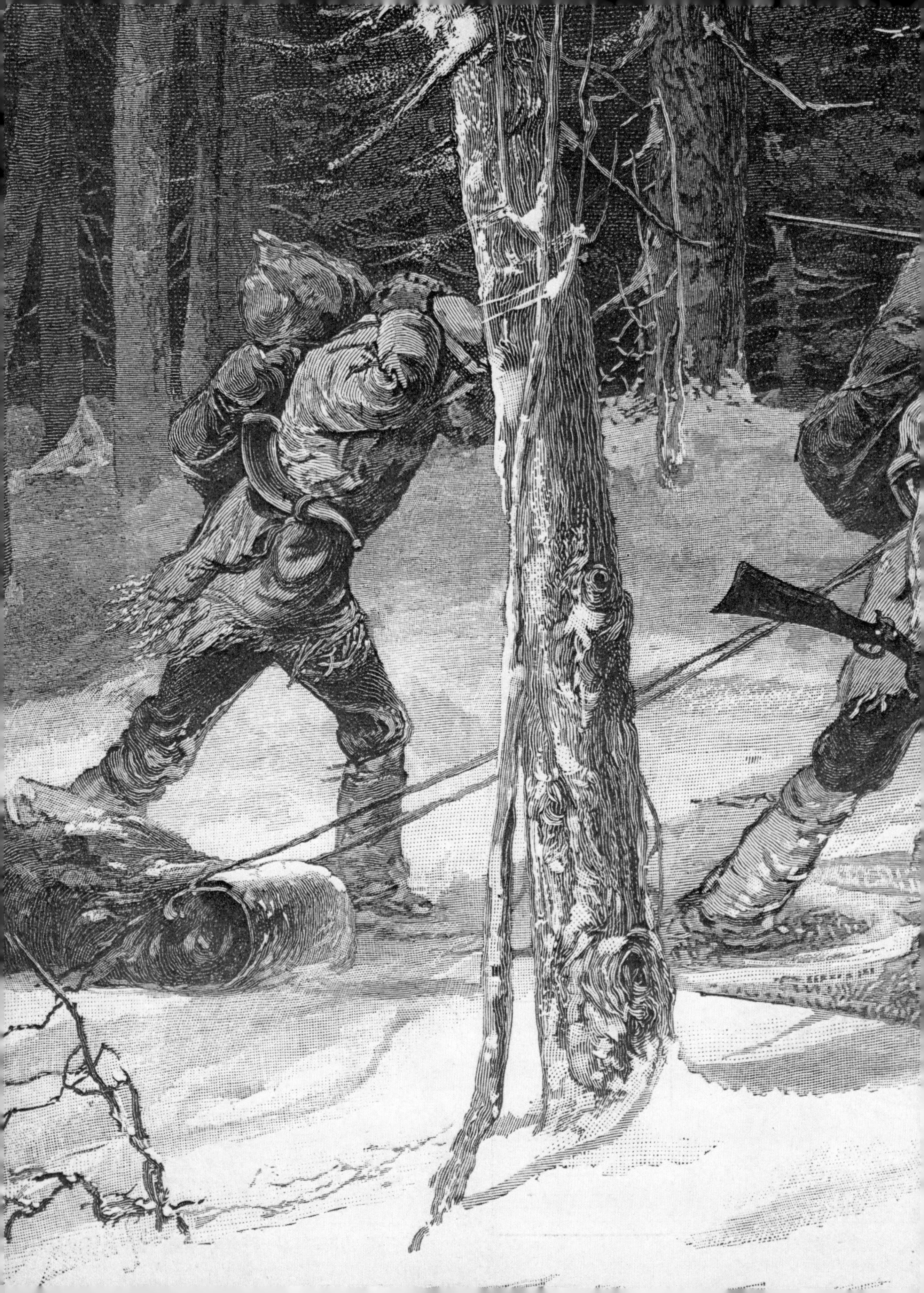

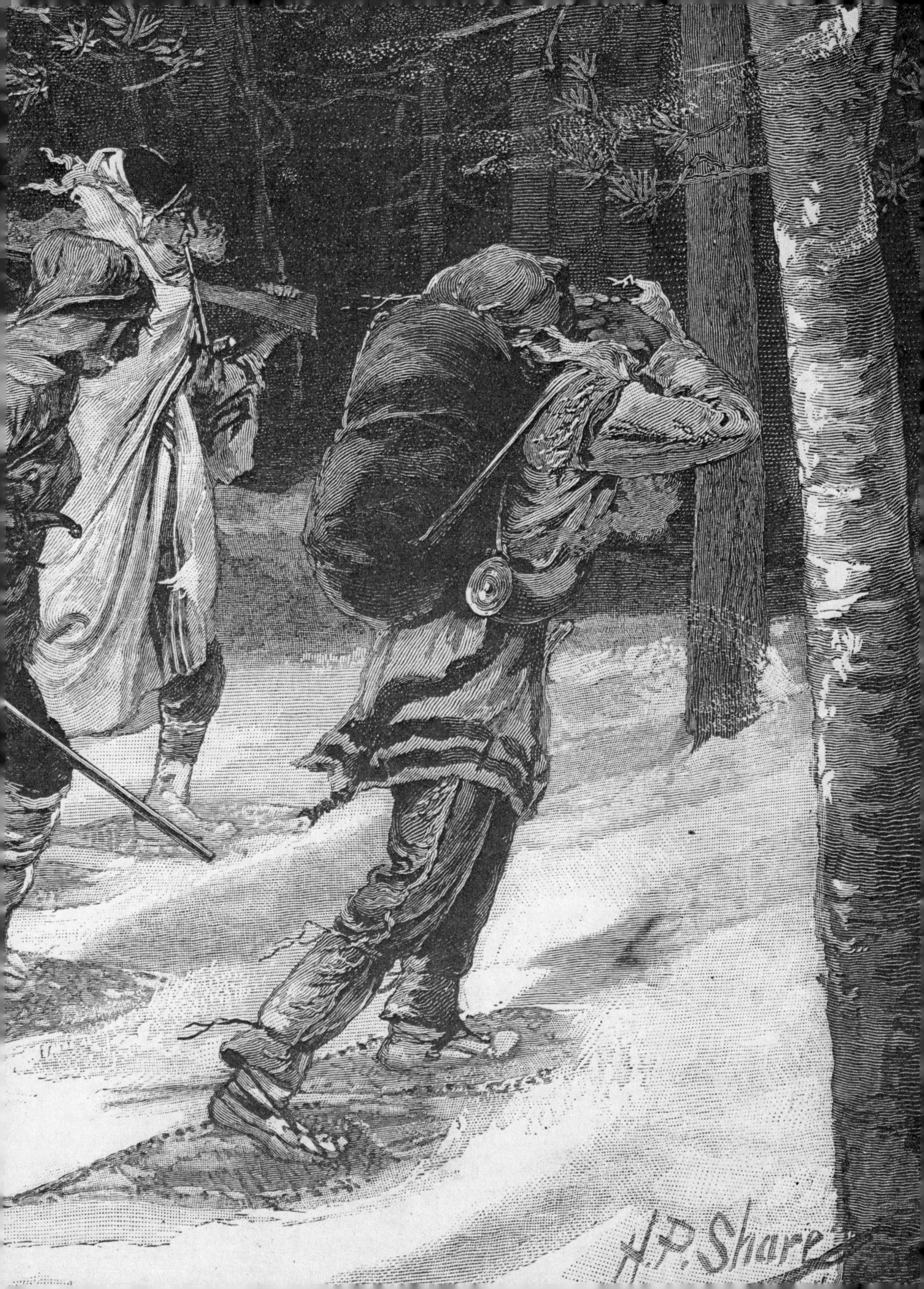
H.P. Share

FUR COATS FOR SPORTSMEN.

"At the International Fur Store you can get a really good and serviceable Fur-lined Overcoat, trimmed with fur collar and cuffs, for £10.

"The more expensive kinds, of course, are Sealskin, Otter, and Beaver. For Racing, Hunting, Coursing, Fishing, and Driving, nothing more comfortable can be worn than Fur or Fur-lined Coats, which can be readily made to do duty as wraps, rugs, &c. To those susceptible to cold, they are really a necessity.

"At the International Fur Store there is the finest collection of Fur and Fur-lined Garments in London, either for Ladies or Gentlemen, and the prices quoted will be found lower than at any other house."—
Sporting Life.

THE INTERNATIONAL FUR STORE,
163 & 198, REGENT STREET,
LONDON, W.

showed no slackening. The returns for dealers in London in 1895 give some idea of the enormous quantity of furs of all sorts passing through their hands, and these all wild: 3,000,000 squirrel pelts; 3,250,000 musk rats from North America; 1,500,000 opossums from Australia and America; 1,500,000 hare skins from Russia, and more from Germany, Greece and Sicily. There were 60,000 beaver skins, for the most part from Canada; 100,000 nutria pelts from South America; 150,000 marmots; 250,000 foxes; 50,000 wolves; 22,000 American otters; 40,000 cats; 30,000 bears and several thousand musk ox skins.

Formidable as these figures are, it is loss of habitat in the face of growing populations which now pose the worst threat to fur-bearing species. While near-war was waging between the Northwest Company and the Hudson's Bay Company on the North American continent and the beaver was just holding his own, another species was being hunted close to extinction further north.

In the spring of 1741 the Russian, Vitus Bering, and his naturalist companion, George Steller, had been engaged on an expedition sponsored by the Czar of all the Russias to explore the strait between the Old and the New Worlds. They had set sail in two ships, the *St Peter* and the *St Paul*, but the *St Paul* had become separated—and was lost to a man. The *St Peter* too was in a poor way, for she had been battered by gales, with a near mutinous crew, and Bering himself now on his third expedition to this inhospitable part of the world was a sick and disillusioned man. He died on 8 December. The *St Peter* was thoroughly lost and now faced with a winter in the terrible waters of the Arctic. As a culmination to their misfortunes the ship ran aground, but it was possible to unload her stores before she broke up in the winter storms.

The crew now found themselves on an island, but it was far from the barren desolate place they had feared, for it abounded in wildlife. To the naturalist Steller it was a paradise of ptarmigan, sea birds and ducks, seals and sea lions. A strange animal with the most lustrous fur swam in the shallow waters—the sea-otter. And wallowing on the shore was the most remarkable creature they had ever seen. This was Steller's sea-cow a member of the same family as the manatee which was known in the West Indies and Caribbean. But whereas that creature was around seven to 12 feet long and weighed around 500 lbs, this strange animal was vastly bigger at nearly 23 feet and weighed well over ten times more than its Caribbean cousins. It was as well that Steller made such meticulous measurements of the enormous, gluttonous, inoffensive beast for 27 years later, in 1768, what was believed to have been the last of Steller's sea-cows was killed by the Russian sealers.

The survivors from the *St Peter* returned to civilization the following year, bringing back tales of the wonderful animals they had seen, and a handsome number of sea-otter pelts. Soon the sealers which coursed the waters of the Bering Strait for the fur-seals would call on their way to and from the sealing grounds to take their toll of sea-otters.

With China ready to take any number of sea-otter furs, the Russians set up the Russian-American Company to try to resolve order out of what was fast becoming a fur free-for-all. Soon British and American hunters vied with the Russians for the lucrative sea-otter trade with the Orient. In 1801 a fleet of 15 American ships was engaged in sole trade in sea-otter skins with China. In 1856 the Russian-American Company sold 118,000 sea-otter skins. In 1885 the figure was down to 8,000 and in 1910, a bare 400 and each skin was selling for a fabulous sum. The species was then protected, but the protection appeared to be an empty gesture for it was feared that the sea-otter had followed Steller's sea-cow into total extinction. The sea-otter was forgotten. Then in 1938 a strange creature was spotted swimming off the coast of North California. Could this be the legendary sea-otter? Closer inspection showed that there were no less than five small colonies of the engaging creature in the immediate area. Since then the sea-otter has gone from strength to strength and the present population is believed to be over 50,000 in Alaskan waters, and some 2,000 on the shores of California and the north-west states of America.

The engaging sea-otter which was once almost hunted to extinction.

The sea-otter was not the only Arctic animal sought for its skin in those bloody years of the last century. The fur seal with its immensely valuable pelt has always been a prime target for fur hunters. And from

Hunting the walrus among the ice floes of Arctic waters.

1800 there took place a systematic extermination of fur seals across the North Pacific waters. The monopoly of the Russian-American Company created some order out of chaos, but still both male and female seals were being killed in a species which produces young only every two years—a warrant for total extermination. In 1806 a moratorium was imposed for two years on Russian seal killing, but it was of little effect and the seal herds diminished year by year. Between the years 1871–90 115,000 seals were slaughtered and by 1912 the fur seal was facing extinction.

Fur seals breed in two groups. One is to be found in the Russian Komandorskiye Islands in the Bering Sea, the other on the Pribilof Islands where the survivors of Bering's expedition had found sanctuary.

Much of the killing of the fur seals went on in the breeding grounds, but more detrimental to the surviving stocks was pelagic killing (killing on the seas). The American sealing fleet was over 100 vessels strong by that time. Sailing from California and the Pacific ports of the west coast of America they would intercept the great herds of fur-seals returning to their breeding grounds in the Pribilof Islands and then follow them to the Bering Sea spearing or shooting the seals as they sailed among them on the way north. It was wasteful as only half of the seals were ever recovered, the rest sank. It was also potentially disastrous for it was impossible to tell the male from the female seals. Not content, the sealers then cruised in the Bering Seas killing in the feeding grounds. The beaches of the Pribilofs became a graveyard of seal pups whose mothers had been killed and where they had starved to death. In 1912 with the fur-seal facing extinction, at last the governments acted. It was none too soon; in 1867, when the United States purchased Alaska from Russia, the population of seals was estimated at between two and a half and four million. In 1912 it was no more than 150,000. In 1912, though, a 15 year ban on all pelagic killing of fur-seals was agreed by the American, British (on behalf of the Canadians), Russian and Japanese governments; further, all seal killing on shore would from thenceforth be government controlled. Now an average of between 30,000 and 60,000 seals are culled every year.

Seals are highly polygamous, therefore any herd is bound to have an excess of males. It is the bachelors who are culled and the stocks of fur-seal have, after an uneasy history and near extinction only 70 years ago, now found their own level. It is a classic case of how intelligent game management has not only saved a species, but has saved the livelihood of a considerable community of hunters who otherwise would have been denied the only way of life they knew.

Indiscriminate slaughter almost wiped out the fur seals on the Alaskan Pribilof Islands.

Fur-bearing animals have been the principal victims of man's extinction process since the earliest days of civilization. Over the years, and even today, the demand for furs has remained enormous and doubtless fur stocks would have been stripped had it not been for the discovery that certain species could be bred in captivity, not only satisfactorily, but with greater certainty than in the wild. The first mink farms were established in the United States in 1866, and a fur farm on Prince Edward Island in Canada in 1894 made successful pioneer experiments with red and silver foxes in an attempt to produce a true breeding strain. Then in 1923 a remarkable operation was put in train to rescue the beautiful chinchilla from extermination.

The chinchilla is a small member of the rodent family, its habitat is in the higher reaches of the Andes, in Bolivia, Chile and Peru, and although only nine inches long it possesses one of the softest and most delicate furs in existence.

The Incas made use of chinchilla hair to weave a very soft cloth and its skins, which were so thin and delicate that they had to be worked with exquisite care, went to line their mantles and cloaks. The Spaniards duly sent back a large number of chinchilla furs, and so highly appreciated were they in the courts of Europe that they were known as the royal fur. For over 350 years the chinchilla was hunted for its fur and in 1895 no less than 400,000 pelts were exported from Chile alone and it soon became clear that the animal was very close to being wiped out. At a critical moment the governments in South America acted and the taking of chinchillas was made illegal.

After the First World War an American mining engineer, Matthias Chapman, who had been working in Chile conceived the idea of starting chinchilla fur farms. He obtained the permission of the Chilean government to take some breeding stock back to the United States, but it was to take him five years before he could at last acquire four males and seven females. The journey to the coast took a further three years to allow the little creatures time to acclimatize themselves to change of altitude and temperature. The journey to California took a further 40 days and during the crossing of the Equator the chinchillas were kept in ice. They arrived in Los Angeles in the depth of winter and as this coincided with their natural time of moult they arrived shivering, nearly naked and wrapped in blankets and hot-water bottles. But amazingly they all survived and this remarkable rescue operation provided the breeding stock for the chinchilla ranches which keep the market supplied with this remarkable fur.

Another animal which the Incas of Peru hunted was the vicuna, one of the four members of the camel family indigenous to South America—the others being the guanaco, the llama and the alpaca. The llama and alpaca have been domesticated since the pre-Inca era, but most efforts to domesticate the vicuna, the smallest of the four species, have failed. In fact, domestication is uneconomic, for the vicuna only yields up to half a pound of wool, but this is of such superlative quality that it has proved worthwhile for hunters to penetrate the vicuna's habitat in the higher reaches of the Andes in the hunt for the animal.

The Incas were fully conscious of the value of vicuna wool and it was

The South American chinchilla, whose coat was regarded as the royal fur, saved from extinction. Illustration by Carl Pitwon.

The vicuna, almost wiped out by fur hunters.

reserved for the use of only the Inca. From time to time a royal hunt, the *chaco*, would be mounted. In this up to 30,000 men would be employed and surrounding a huge area, up to 50 miles across, they would start to converge driving all the animals before them. Deer and lesser animals would be killed for meat, the vicuna would be taken alive, shorn of their wool and released. Each area was cropped every three to five years. It was a highly efficient method of game cropping and permitted the vicuna to recover and grow its fleece before the next *chaco*.

Such orderliness came to an abrupt end with the arrival of the Spaniard and from that time the gradual erosion of the vicuna population can be measured. Its original habitat included Ecuador, Peru, Bolivia and northern Chile and north-west Argentina. It is wiped out now in all but isolated populations in Peru and some in Bolivia.

Attempts at preserving the vicuna were put in hand as long ago as 1825 by Simon Bolivar, the 'Liberator', but these proved unsatisfactory. For nearly 100 years from then the vicuna lived in comparative peace in its Andean fastnesses. But so remote were its habitats that the population remained almost untouched. The arrival of modern communications and firearms saw a rapid end to that happy state of affairs and the 1960s saw an astonishing slaughter for vicuna skins.

It is estimated that in the ten years between 1957 and 1967 a population of close on 500,000 head—half of which were in Peru—was reduced to an astonishing 15,000 in Peru and less than 1,000 in Bolivia. The vicuna is now a wholly protected species.

The shooting of spotted cats depicted by George Catlin, the American artist in Brazil. Spotted cats have long been sought for their fur.

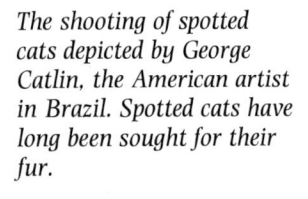

The 1960s was a highly significant period in the saving of many species of fur-bearing animals. It was a time of intense conservation activity and saw the gradual awareness in many quarters of the plight of wildlife and how desperately urgent action was needed if entire species were not to disappear. Perhaps the most important case history concerned the spotted cats.

For as fashion saved the beaver in the last century, it has been fashion that dramatically and in a very few years has gravely threatened the survival of several species of spotted cat.

There had long been a market for spotted cats, the leopard, the cheetah, smaller cats from Africa, the jaguar and ocelot from South America. This had persisted throughout the earlier decades of the present century but there was no boom in spotted cat furs. Suddenly the market for spotted cats exploded. Everyone wanted leopard skin coats, trousers, handbags. With modern methods of hunting and modern weapons the cats were doomed unless very quick international action was put in train. In 1964 no less than 50,000 leopard skins were exported from East Africa.

In 1970, under pressure from the International Union for the Conservation of Nature and Natural Resources (IUCN), a total embargo was placed by the International Fur Trade on handling the skins of the tiger, the Great and La Plata otters from South America, the beautiful clouded and snow leopards from the Himalayas and a moratorium placed on the sale of cheetah and leopard skins. This was the start of increasingly stringent restrictions intended to curb the trade in rare or endangered species, but these measures dealt only with legal and legitimate export. A flourishing black market exists in these furs, and as long as this continues there will be nothing to prevent hunting even to the point of extinction if by taking one cat a hunter can earn more than his entire annual wage.

Only drastic and effective international action can save several species of spotted cat. The jaguar.

The Passing of the Buffalo

It is a sentimental error to legislate in favour of the bison. You should, on the contrary, congratulate the skin hunters and give each of them a bronze medal with on one side the image of a dead bison and on the other that of a distressed Indian. The hide hunters have done more to solve the Indian problem than the whole of the American Army in thirty years. The extermination of the bison is the only way of founding a lasting peace and of favoring the progress of civilization.

General Sheridan

Buffalo hunting, by the great illustrator of North American Indian life George Catlin.

The first white men to see the North American bison (or as it incorrectly and universally came to be called—the buffalo) on its native Middle West plains were the Spaniards pushing northwards from the Gulf of Mexico, but it was not unknown even then for as early as 1521 Cortez had come across what he called the Mexican Bull in the menagerie of the Aztec king, Montezeuma. 'A wonderful composition of divers animals', a chronicler accompanying the expedition described it, 'It has crooked shoulders, with a Bunch on its back like a Camel, its flanks dry, its tail large, and its neck covered with hair like a Lion. It is cloven-footed, its head armed like that of a Bull, which it resembles in fierceness, with no less strength and agility.' Indeed the appearance of the buffalo is faintly ridiculous. 'There is a mixture of the awful and the comic in the look of these huge animals,' described Washington Irving. 'They have their great bulk forward with an up-and-down motion of the unwieldy head and shoulders. Their tails cock up like a queue of Pantaloon in pantomime, in the end whisking about in a fierce yet whimsical expression of fright and fury.'

The 'awful and comic' North American bison (after an illustration by Father Louis Hennepin).

In the Middle Ages the buffalo was to be found across most of North America. Many of the great American highways follow age-old buffalo routes across the landscape and through the mountains. But the buffalo was incompatible with the spread of civilization. It could not be domesticated like the forebears of the farmers' and settlers' cattle. Those who tried found that the calves were docile and tractable up to the age of 12 months or so, but thereafter the growing animals became increasingly unreliable and unpredictable. Worse still, they ate grazing suitable for domestic beef, and so heavy was the beast that no fence could keep them out, or in—even the barbed wire fence which made its appearance in the 1850s was no match for even a half-grown buffalo. East of the Mississippi, by 1800, barely a single buffalo remained—the last believed killed in 1825.

If the buffalo was an inconvenience and an embarrassment to the white man and doomed to elimination in the interests of progress and advancement, to the American Indian of the plains the animal was his life blood. The first American settlers had crossed from Siberia 40,000 years ago. These early Americans had followed the great herds of large grass-eating mammoths, musk oxen, moose and several species of bison when they moved southwards to escape the hardships of a northern winter. In their time and in their own primitive but highly effective way they had eliminated the survivors, leaving their own descendants to hunt the prairies and forests, subsisting on what the Great Spirit provided—and the most bountiful of all the Great Spirit's

Buffalo herds at sunset illustrated by Gustav Doré.

gifts was the buffalo. Buffalo worship was important in many religious ceremonies in the tribal ritual of the Plains Indians, who knew, recognized and were grateful for the apparently unending supply of all they needed to exist and thrive on. According to a legend of the Kiowa tribe the Great Spirit had announced, 'Here are the buffalo, they shall be your food and your raiment, but in the day that you shall see them perish from off the face of the Earth, then know that the end of the Kiowas is near and the sun set.'

But nothing appeared less likely to an Indian eye as he beheld the vast herds of peacefully browsing buffalo as they moved like a 'great brown blanket' across the country. To the Indian the buffalo was a mystery. Some believed that they were produced in fabulous numbers underground in great caves in the winter and came forth when the prairie began to change colour from dingy brown to the pale green of rejuvenating life. Others thought of them as vanishing underground beneath a mighty lake to the north—and if one listened hard enough it was possible to discern the tramp tramp of their countless thousand hooves as they roamed restlessly under the ground, waiting for the great thaw and growth to begin again.

The buffalo dance of the Mandan Indians by Karl Bodmer.

The buffalo provided all the Indian needed. The skin—the robe, as it was known—was his winter covering; the skinned hide would make fine mocassins and belts. The tough thick folds of the neck would, when it was shrunken, dried and flattened, make a shield to protect him from any arrow, and most musket balls, when of double thickness it would turn any bullet except that of the great guns the buffalo hunters later used. The huge shoulder blades of the buffalo could be turned into axes and the sharper bones used to scrape hides. Little was wasted; the hooves crushed down to make glue, the magnificent sinews along the back were fine bow strings, the hair when twisted made ropes and cords, the little tail an admirable fly whisk. The droppings, buffalo chips, were excellent and often the only fuel available—it was said to give a

Hunted in the water . . .

certain rather peppery taste to the meat, for the flesh was delicious. The Indian speciality was pemmican, made by drying thin strips of flesh, pounding it almost to powder and mixing it with buffalo fat. It was then poured into lengths of the intestine, into boxes or bags, with berries to give extra flavour—a complete food which kept well during even the hottest days, nourishing and pronounced delicious by all who tasted it.

As a rule the Indian was not wasteful. He killed only what he needed, leaving the rest of the herd to increase and multiply. His killing methods varied. Sometimes the buffalo herds would be driven into a pound or stockade where those trapped inside could be slaughtered at leisure for use in the hard months. In winter the great creatures would crash through the snow drifts and be helpless before the arrow or lance of the pursuing hunter. Occasionally the Indian would resort to fire to trap the buffalo and surrounded by flame and blinded by smoke the panic-stricken beasts would be easy prey.

. . . or in the snow (George Catlin).

The buffalo provided all the Indian needed (George Catlin).

Requiring more skill was the riding kill—the chase on horseback by some of the finest horsemen in the world. Even the short 30 ins bows with razor-sharp arrows were powerful enough to transfix two buffalo and an arrow placed behind the ribs into heart, lung or intestinal cavity was enough to kill. It was a dangerous game, for the apparently blundering buffalo could turn like lightning and with one twist of the mighty head with its razor-like horns rip open a horse. Little the wonder that the best buffalo horses, as light on their feet as ballet dancers and long experienced in the ways of the buffalo, were highly prized.

The great buffalo herds were easily alarmed and stampeded. Storms, lightning or fire were the most common causes. But sometimes an undetectable and unknown agency might set off a communal panic and once on the move there was no stopping them. Those who witnessed a buffalo stampede remembered it as the most terrifying experience of their lives. One, Hepwood Dickson, an early traveller to the Middle West, wrote:

> The black, shaggy beasts continued to thunder past us in handfuls, in groups, in masses, in whole armies; for forty hours in succession we never lost sight of them, thousands upon thousands, tens of thousands upon tens of thousands, a numberless multitude of

untamed creatures, whose meat, as we thought, would be sufficient to supply the wigwams of the Indians to all eternity.

Waggon trains caught in the line of such a stampede had little chance, all that remained after the buffalo had passed was the sorry mess that had once been human beings and splinters little larger than matchwood of their waggons pounded to pieces by countless thousand hooves.

Not even the trains on the railroads which began to push westwards over the continent were immune. An army officer wrote:

> We entered a large herd which scattered and seemed to go wild at the shrieking of the whistle and the ringing of the bell. As we went on the thicker they became, until the very earth appeared to be a rolling mass of humps as far as we could see. Suddenly some of the animals nearest us turned and charged, others fell in behind, and down on us they came like an avalanche. The engineer stopped the engine, let off steam and whistled to stop them, while we fired from the platforms and windows. We stood in the center of the car to avert the crash. On they came, the earth trembling, and plunged head down into us. Some even wedged in between the cars, others beneath, and so great was the crash that they toppled three cars over and actually scrambled over them, one buffalo becoming bogged by having his legs caught in the window.

The inroads made by the hunting forays of the Plains Indians took a heavy toll of the buffalo herds. The scavenging wolves and other predators which followed the herds to pick off the young, the weak and the ailing accounted for more, but helped maintain the quality of the herd. Fire was a grave danger on the prairie and many a herd blundered to its death in panic-stricken flight. Each spring an astonishing number, used to crossing the ice in mid-winter when it could bear their weight, would drown as the melting ice gave way beneath them. Thousands of corpses at a time would be washed down the rivers and streams setting up a stink which could be smelled half a mile or more away. But even these catastrophes, man-made or natural, had no real effect on the buffalo population.

Buffalo were so plentiful that whenever civilization tried to take root they became a menace. Garrison orders for a fort in the Middle West laid down that 'Members of the Command will, when shooting buffaloes on the parade ground, be careful not to fire in the direction of the Commanding Officer's quarters!' The early telegraph poles soon fell victim to the buffalo habit of scratching. When an astute telegraph engineer, exasperated with constantly replacing his poles hammered in nails and spikes to discourage the habit, the buffalo found this even more to their liking.

1. The start.
2. On the lookout.
3. Slaughter from the railway train.
4. Sport of the past.
5. In camp.
6. Bone hunters.
7. Creeping up to the game.
8. A herd in a "blizzard."
9. Bone heaps and hide-press alongside the railway.

Buffalo Hunting in North America.

FROM SKETCHES BY P. FRENZENY.

69

It was never known, it was beyond computation, how many buffalo there were at the turn of the nineteenth century. Some reckon 50 million, others put the figure as high as 65 million. By 1830 however, it was thought that some 40 million buffalo still ranged the plains. But what is indisputable is that in an incredible 13 years, from 1870 to 1883, millions of buffalo simply disappeared, slaughtered until only a few scattered remnants were left in private herds or in Yellowstone National Park, and these numbered no more than a few hundred.

But these days were far in the future. In 1868 a traveller could pass through many mid-western states for weeks at a time and never be out of sight of buffalo. For buffalo country stretched for 1,500 miles from the Colorado River in Texas in the south and well into Canada at its northern end—a strip of North America 500 miles wide. In this territory lived four enormous congregations of buffalo. Following their practice to graze into the wind these populations ranged in gigantic circles 300–400 miles across, southerly in winter, northerly in summer when the lush buffalo-grass was at its best.

For years the Indians had carried on a trade in buffalo robes, beaver and other furs. But by comparison with those from further north, the beaver they provided was a poor article. So increasingly they came to depend on the robe as their principal trading article. They also—as the beaver did elsewhere—became the Indian's currency. Ten caps of sugar was equivalent to one buffalo robe; ten robes for one pony; three ponies for a tepee. Sometimes the Indians would gather in great buffalo hunts employing 300–400 warriors and killing upwards of 1,000 head. Such killing in the early decades of the last century soon started to make inroads into buffalo stocks, and by 1850 buffalo were becoming scarce in some areas. It was a foretaste of one of the most remarkable episodes in man's war against animals.

The sheer inaccessibility of the great plains, though, meant that the vast herds in most of the Middle West were untouched until the building of the railroads. In 1862 a bill was passed for the construction of a railroad from the western borders of Iowa to San Francisco. In 1865 work on the Union Pacific Railroad commenced and two years later had reached Cheyenne. The principal mass of buffalo were thus neatly divided. Those to the south of the railroad became known as the South herd, largely centred around the Republican River between Arkansas and South Platte. In the general area bounded by the Powder River to the Canadian border lived the somewhat smaller North herd.

In 1871 Wyatt Earp, as fine an outdoorsman and buffalo hunter as he became upholder of the law in those lawless days, described his experiences:

The ground on which I stood was the highest point within miles. Before me, to the west and south, the prairies rolled in a series of small mounds and wide, level stretches pitted with buffalo wallows as far as

I could see, twenty or thirty miles in each direction. For all that distance the range seemed literally packed with grazing buffaloes. The animals were feeding in the customary bunches of twenty to two hundred, and in the foreground the open spaces between them were plainly evident. But in the middle distance the prairie appeared to be covered by a solid mass of huge, furry heads and humps, flowing slowly along like a great muddy river. Beyond the point where I could make out individual animals or groups, I remember thinking that the rolling plains, which I knew were treeless had by some freak been covered with a growth of stunted, dark shrubbery. Clear to the horizon the herd was endless.

Earp and his companion reckoned that there were upwards of one million beasts in this one herd, a figure also arrived at by an army party which had come upon them from a different direction. Seven years later Wyatt Earp passed the same way again, this time there was not a single buffalo to be found.

For the previous 20 years before the railroads were completed, the robe trade had been building in importance. It has been estimated that some 200,000 were annually reaching eastern markets from about

Mark Twain referred to men such as these as 'dismal hunters . . . wearing weapons of defense and offense, carrying parlors upon wheels, kitchens in their carts, shooting rabbits, and Indians as the seasons vary and dining upon the buffalo and corn bread à volunté.'

WANTON DESTR

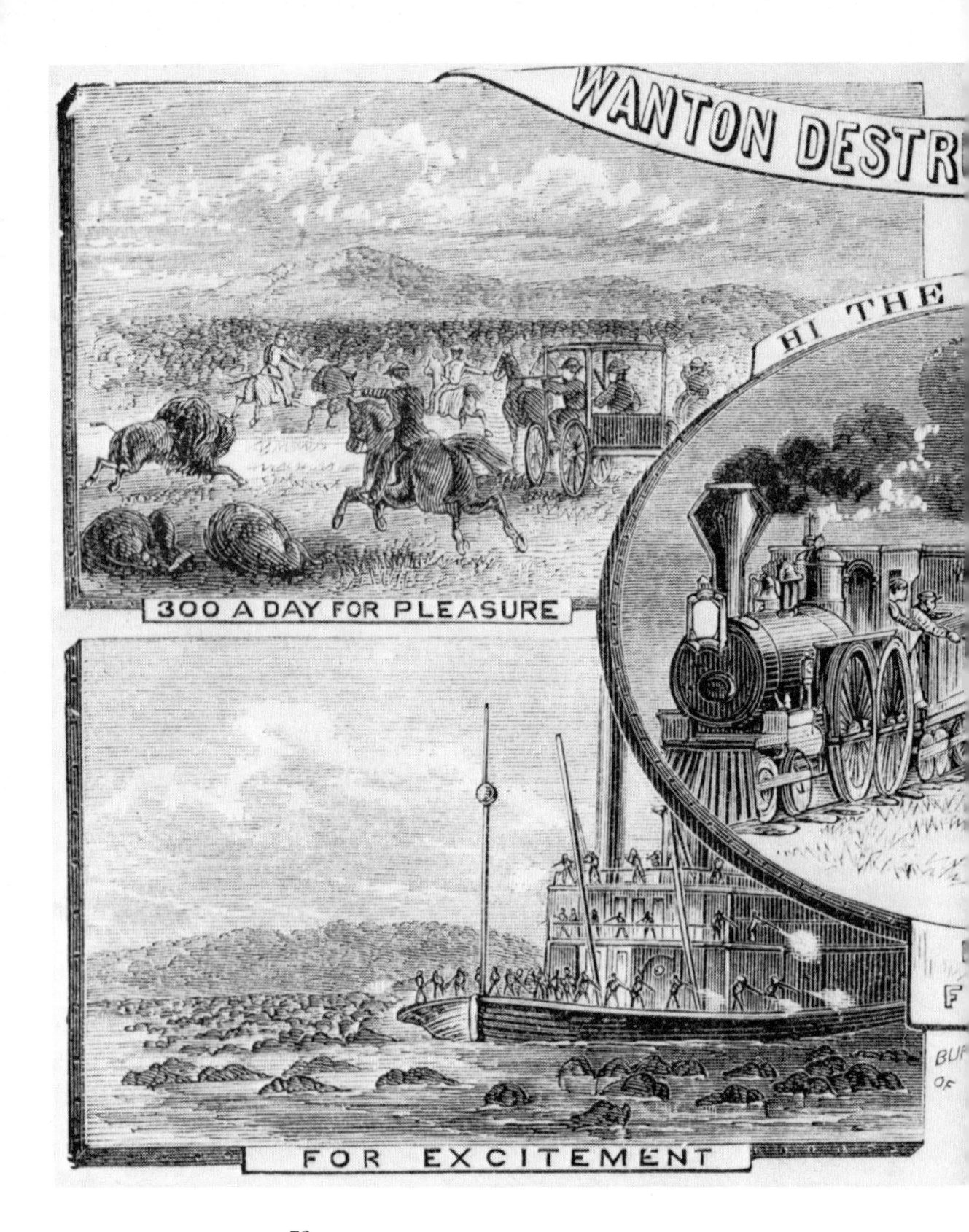

HI THE

300 A DAY FOR PLEASURE

FOR EXCITEMENT

Outcry against the buffalo slaughter gathered strength—but it was a small voice against powerful vested interests.

1840 onwards, but this was a wasteful process as these were probably the end product of between seven and ten times that number of buffalo. Then in 1870 a method of curing buffalo hide rather than the robe was developed by a German tannery company. The technique was passed to British and eastern American tanneries and the great slaughter was ready to begin. The following year the Atchison, Topeka and Santa Fé railroad crossed the state of Kansas and now at last the mass of buffalo could be reached by the guns of the professional hunter who, in their hundreds and later in their thousands, set about the task of extermination.

All across Kansas, Nebraska, Wyoming and Texas the sight of great piles of hides awaiting shipment to the east became common. The heavy overpowering all-pervading smell of curing hides hung like a pall over the booming towns of the Middle West and for miles on either side of the small townships they were to be seen stretched on the ground drying in the sun. The feeding of the railroad construction gangs on buffalo meat, a contract which had involved W. F. Cody—Buffalo Bill—of legendary Wild West and later circus fame, killing over 4,000 buffalo in 18 months, had at least used most of the meat on the great animal, but the hide hunter needed nothing more than the skin.

The buffalo tongue was a delicacy fit for a gourmet and tongues, fresh in winter or smoked at any time of the year, were sent in their thousands for the tables of the city dwellers in the eastern states. The 'fleece' on either side of the backbone was a particularly tasty morsel. The hump was another. Perhaps the total of these choice cuts and the tongue amounted to some 100–150 lbs of meat, but that was all from an animal of nearly 2,000 lbs. The plain was littered with the whitening, stinking carcases skinned and then abandoned to be feast for carrion.

It was a free-for-all of the most horrific nature. The killing was, as one witness described, 'a rage of slaughter'. The buffalo seemed to exert a fascination for the hunter and would-be hunter. They were easy to hit, they were not even hard to kill. There was no sport, no danger and little skill needed for the long-range pot-shotting which most indulged in. But somehow the buffalo seemed to bring out man's primaeval killing instinct. 'What man could resist the temptation, when the whole earth it seemed was a surging, trembling mass of these animals,' wrote one exultant hunter.

Shooting from trains was a popular sport. Some lines ran special excursions, 'guaranteeing' for $10 a head that there would be ample buffalo within easy shooting range from the cars. When a buffalo was killed the engineer obligingly stopped his locomotive while the lucky marksman dismounted, cut out the tongue and carved off any other joint he might wish, and then continue on his way.

It was a not uncommon occurrence: 'At this moment,' wrote a traveller on one of these excursion trains, 'a shout of "buffalo crossing the track!" was heard, and Bang! Bang! Bang! Simultaneously went

Shooting from a train became a popular sport.

several pieces. Poking my head out of the window I observed a small herd of six buffalo bulls running at full speed parallel with the train, and about a hundred yards ahead and not more than sixty feet from the track.'

One of the two shot buffalo was trying to escape.

> He had been shot in the thigh and though retarded made good progress, when another ball taking effect in the other leg, let his hind quarters down upon the ground. Nothing daunted the wounded animal made every exertion to drag himself off, on his two fore feet, when a ball under his shoulder put an end to his suffering—and his efforts to rejoin his companions ... the busy knives of the 'professionals' in hip-jointing operations, soon had the rumps severed after cutting out the tongue and a few strips of 'hump' the rest of the immense carcase was left as a dainty and abundant repast to the wolves. The meat was put on the train, and again we continued our journey.

The true sportsman's way to kill buffalo was to ride them down. This involved a steady approach downwind—for the smell of horse would create an unstoppable stampede—about 300 yards off the buffalo would start to become restless and move, at 250 yards the movement would become a mad dash and then was the time to go. It required a steady nerve and a steadier seat, as well as a constant awareness that your horse might swerve suddenly or tread in one of the many gopher holes. As the Indian would use an arrow, so the white man could kill with a revolver, there was no better weapon than Mr Colt's six-shooter. An area one foot square behind the ribs was the lethal mark, any shot there would result in a kill. The skilled might delay their shot in the sheer exultation of the chase. General Custer once wrote: 'Repeatedly could I have placed the muzzle of my revolver against the shaggy body of the huge beast, yet each time would I withdraw the weapon, as if to prolong the excitement of the race. Mile after mile was traversed in this way.'

This was the day of the muzzle-loading rifle. There was no time to use the ramrod to push home the charge. Instead the hunter would prime from his pocket, drop a bullet down the barrel from his mouth, a quick tap on the saddle to knock the ball home and he was ready. If he pointed his weapon down towards the ground then the bullet rolled out. This led to shooting with the rifle lying across the saddle and at full gallop. For sport or killing for meat, riding down was satisfactory. But for the hide hunters it was wearisome having to move from one carcase to another sometimes several miles apart, it was also time-wasting. Thus developed the lethal 'stand'.

No method of killing could rival the lethal 'stand' when a skilled hunter could shoot dozens of the placid incurious buffaloes without moving.

The great blundering buffalo suffered from severe near-sightedness. In the herd, except at what was called running time when the bulls roared and bellowed in their fight for supremacy, they appeared placid and uncurious. Soon enough hunters discovered that with a bit of guile they could shoot more than one buffalo without the rest of the herd becoming alarmed. At first the weapons they used were too small to allow for long-range shooting. Then, a gunsmith, Christian Sharps, introduced his .50 calibre breech-loading rifle. With a slug of lead two inches by half an inch the Big Fifty or 'Ole Pizen Slinger'—as the hide hunters called it with affection—a massive weapon weighing in the order of 18 lbs, had a lethal range of up to one mile. But for closer shooting, with the Big Fifty propped up on tripod or forked stick a skilled hunter could kill in a 'stand' on an unprecedented scale. According to one veteran hunter:

> Only skilled hunters could hold a bunch of buffs in a Stand. The leader, usually an old cow, would be watched by the others in the herd near her, probably with an idea of running if she would lead the way, but without initiative to start a stampede. They would see her standing still and would resume their grazing. The wounded cow would wobble, then stagger forward and fall. Watching the herd carefully, I would note any movement on the part of any buffalo to take fright and start off. That would be my next victim. It would begin bleeding, lurching unsteadily, and would fall. Several would walk up and sniff the two on the ground. They would throw up their heads and bawl, and one or two might start off. Then I must drop them. Sometimes a whole bunch would start. Then I must shoot quickly, dropping the leader. That would turn the others back. The idea was to keep the buffaloes milling around in a restricted spot, shooting those on the outskirts that tried to move away.

A hunter might shoot 60 or 70 buffalo during one stand, if he was lucky and skilful. The record was 107, but stands of 40 or 50 were so common as to be unremarked.

The hide trade became big business.

In an incredible 13 years nearly 10,000,000 buffaloes were slaughtered. Soon nothing but bones were left of the once great herds—and even these found a ready market.

In 1871 the hide trade began in earnest. The market for hides cured in the new way was massive, and it was a trade that could be carried on the year round. No longer sacred was the summer rest, when the robes were at their worst, or the running period when the herds were unapproachable and the buffalo spared from the otherwise almost constant slaughter. Now the boom of the big guns echoed across the prairie, month in and month out.

The demand for hides in England and further afield was avid as the new leather was more elastic and stronger than most others on the market. Furniture covered with buffalo hide, wall panelling, and linings for coach and carriage used an incredible quantity of skins. It was still wasteful, not only of the meat left to rot, but also because many hides were unsaleable due to rot or beetle. Occasionally, wolves damaged the skins pinned on the ground or Indians, resentful at seeing what they looked on as their livelihood disappearing, attacked the hide hunters. Few people were concerned that the buffalo herds appeared to be becoming less numerous. The professional buffalo hunters, the hide men, the meat men and the tongue men, all carved away at buffalo populations. The plainsmen thought that no amount of killing could possibly make permanent inroads into the vast herds. The hide men, if they thought about it at all, didn't care. This was a very lucrative business, and they were out to make the best of it while stocks lasted. In the years 1872 and 1873, 1,500,000 hides were carried by the three railroads which transfixed buffalo territory.

The Big Fifty, and other newer and more lethal weapons, some now fitted with telescopic sights, killed as many buffalo as the skinners could comfortably handle. And when one herd was dealt with and the remainder had run off in panic, the skinners went to work. Around the camp fire in the evening they would talk and reminisce without fear for the future, or so they thought:

> *When the day's hunt is over, and all have had their dinners,*
> *The hunter lights his pipe, to entertain the skinners,*
> *He tells of the big bull that bravely met its fate,*
> *Of the splendid line shot that settled its mate;*
> *Of the cow, shot too low, of another shot too high,*
> *And of all the shots that missed he tells the reason why,*
> *How the spike stood his ground, when all but him had fled,*
> *And he refused to give it up until he filled him with lead,*
> *How he travelled up the trail for five miles or more,*
> *Leaving over forty victims weltering in their gore.*

As the plains of Kansas emptied of buffalo and the South herd began to be whittled away, the hunters moved into Indian territory. Game laws had by then been proposed by a number of states to try to call a halt to the killing, but these foundered in Congress. Voices were raised that the elimination of the buffalo might at last bring the Indian to heel. A senator declared that the shooting of all the buffalo would prove 'a means of hastening their sense of dependance upon the products of the soil and their own labors.'

The killing lobby was powerful. The buffalo, they declared, was an impediment to the settling of the West. If it came to a battle between giving grazing to wild buffalo or domesticated longhorn steers there was no doubt that the former must give way. They were a nuisance, they had to be eliminated. 'There is no law which human hands can write, there is no law which Congress of men can enact, that will stay the disappearance of these wild animals before civilisation. They eat grass. They trample the plains. They are as uncivilised as the Indians.' Yet by ordinance of 1787 it had been declared: 'The upmost good faith shall always be observed towards the Indians, their land and property shall never be taken from them without their consent.'

By 1874 Kansas was virtually cleared. In a belated attempt to save something of the last few herds, the directors of the Kansas Pacific Railroad banned the shooting of buffalo from their trains. By then it was too late. With Kansas empty, the great army of hunters and skinners, estimated to be numbered now in their thousands, moved into Texas.

Within two years Texas had followed the example of Kansas. The great South herd was finished, and already 'sportsmen' were being urged to go west before they lost the last opportunity of shooting a wild buffalo. Now it was the turn of the North herd.

Protected by severe winters and the activities of extremely hostile Indians, the hide hunters had largely left alone the North herd while supplies further south continued. Now, in 1880, a strip of country no more than 180 miles wide, from the Wyoming border north to the Missouri River, and from Little Belt Mountains in central Montana eastwards into the Dakotas, the North herd unsuspectingly awaited their doom. For in 1880 the building of the North Pacific Railroad had begun and as the tracks moved westwards, closely in their wake moved the hide hunters. The carriage figures of hides on that railroad reveal their own dismal story. In 1881, 50,000 hides were transported east; the next year a colossal 200,000; in 1883 the total was down to 40,000. In 1884 a bare 300 and in 1885 none at all. The North herd, like the South eight years before, had ceased to exist.

The result was inevitable when one considers that in 1882 it was calculated that there were no less than 5,000 hide hunters and skinners as well as large numbers of Indians taking advantage of the lucrative and what appeared to be a never-ending trade. Chased and chivied from range to range, prevented from getting water by an almost continuous line of camp fires and driven from it when they found an unguarded stream or trickle, the last of the once fine herds was in desperate straits. These were no longer the fine great fat lumbering beasts that Buffalo Bill had killed to provide food for the construction gangs, instead the last of the buffalo were nervy, long-legged, emaciated rangy animals. But they still had hides and driven north the herd was simply shot to death.

The following year the survivors, some 10–20,000 head in an area between Bismarck and the Black Hills, were nearly all slaughtered in a short-lived killing. A little over 1,000 escaped into Indian country and there chief Sitting Bull and his braves—about 1,000 strong—and almost the same number of white hunters, moved in. In two days the entire herd; bulls, cows, calves had been massacred.

Soon only the whitened bones of the vast herds of buffalo that had once roamed the American plains remained, but not for long. Even these relics were collected. For with the elimination of living buffalo, the hunters turned bone scavengers. The better bones were used in the refining of sugar. The older discoloured ones ground down and used as fertiliser. The best bones of all helped to make the fine bone china that graced the drawing rooms of the east. The horns were used for buttons and knife handles. Even the long shaggy hair went to stuffing cushions.

In an amazingly short time:

They fell by thousands
They melted away like smoke!
Mile by mile they retreated westward;
Year by year they moved north and south.
In dust brown clouds;
Each year they descended upon the plains
In endless floods;
Each winter they retreated to the hills
Of the south;
Their going was like the ocean current,
But each spring they stopped a little short —
They were like an ebbing tide!
They came at last to meagre little bands
That never left the hills —
Crawling in sombre files from cañon to cañon —
Now they are gone!

(Hamlin Garland, *Prairie Songs*, 1893)

To the Indians it was totally perplexing. They spoke of the buffalo having gone to the 'great lone land' to the north and thought of them residing in some remote valley from whence, one day they would return in their former numbers. There was no explanation otherwise, for man could never have exterminated them.

> They are tired with so much running. They have had no rest. They have been chased and chased over the rocks and grass of the prairie and their feet are sore, worn down like those of a tender-footed horse. When the buffalo have rested and their feet have grown out again, they will return to us in larger numbers. Stronger, with better robes and fatter than they ever were.

The buffalo were not wholly eliminated. Perhaps a total of a few hundred head were to be found in isolated and scattered communities—although these stragglers were soon at risk from trophy hunters determined to bag a wild buffalo before it was too late. In 1905 the American Bison Society was founded, and they were instrumental in ensuring the survival of the North American species. The bison in the United States and Canada now number over 20,000, and this figure is kept steady. And it is now again possible to shoot a buffalo in America—under carefully regulated conditions. But this is a very far cry from the days when the prairies were 'one robe' of grazing bison.

White Gold

Ivory has been steeped and dyed in blood. Every pound weight has cost the life of a man, woman or child; for every five pounds a hut has been burned, for every two tusks a whole village has been destroyed, every twenty tusks have been obtained at the price of a district with all its people and plantations...

H. M. Stanley, *In Darkest Africa*, 1890

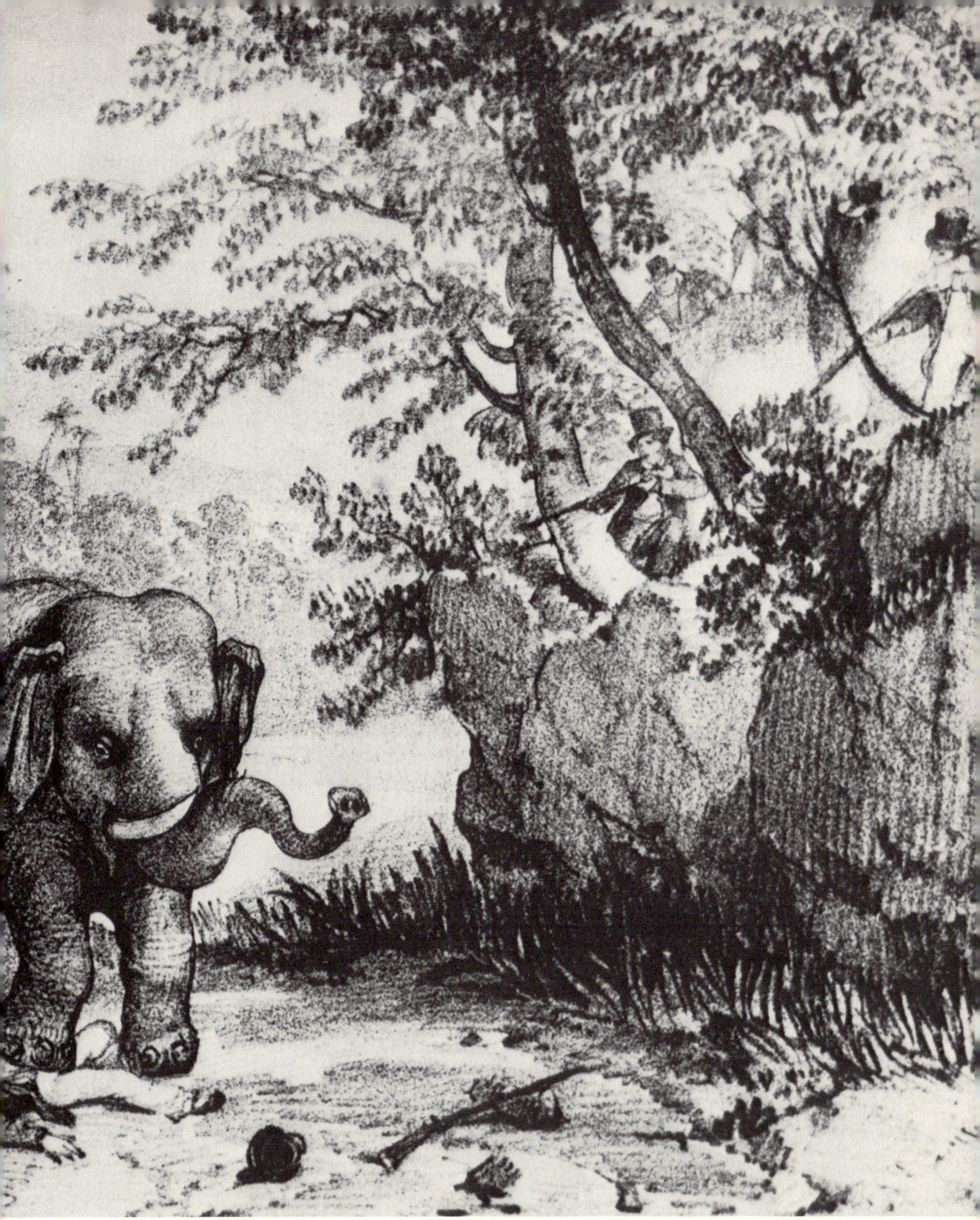

On the 15 September 1885, in the small town of St Thomas in western Ontario, the great African elephant, Jumbo, which had delighted crowds on both sides of the Atlantic for 20 years, was killed by a train. His smaller elephant companion, Tom Thumb, was thrown clear by the impact, but Jumbo met the engine head on, and although he derailed the train he was severely injured. He died holding the hand of his keeper with his trunk. Jumbo was skinned and stuffed and, until 1977, his skeleton stood in the Museum of Natural History in New York.

For elephants hold a unique and sentimental place in our feelings towards the animal world. The great elephant resembles an animal of fiction. Everything about it is peculiar; the waving, immensely muscular trunk, with a highly sensitive tip which can undo knots or turn keys in locks, the vast bulk, the little pig eyes which seem to exhibit a wide range of emotion, the enormous feet and the ridiculous tail added, one might imagine, as an afterthought.

Man's association with elephants goes back for at least 7,000 years.

Hunting the mammoth.

Once great herds of elephant ancestors roamed much of the globe and mammoth remains have been found in North America, in Asia, Europe and Africa. Around 10,000 years ago a great climate change took place in Siberia and wiped out the colossal populations of elephant-type creatures. Sudden death is evident for one specimen was found still with a cud of buttercup in its mouth, and so well preserved have been the remains that mammoth steaks have been cut from the thawed carcase, cooked and found delicious.

In the days of the ancient Greeks and during the early Roman Empire, elephants were to be found in the Near East and along the North African coast, but by the time of the collapse of the Roman Empire there were none west of the River Indus, and they had wholly disappeared from the Moroccan area.

In Asia, though, they were still plentiful, as they had been for several thousand years. Domesticated for centuries, the Asian, or more traditionally, the Indian, elephant was venerated in legend and, if white, worshipped in the flesh. Hindu mythology sees the elephant as holding up the world—in work, in war and in ceremony it has played an important role in the evolution of the southern nations of Asia. In Africa the story has been different.

There are two species of African elephant, the forest elephant, whose range is now confined to the equatorial regions of the Congo basin, and the bush elephant which once ranged much of the rest of Africa south of the Sahara. The forest elephant (Loxodonta africana cyclotis) is some seven to eight feet high at the shoulder and differs from its larger cousin, the bush elephant (Loxodonta africana), in having fewer toenails on either foot and possessing tusks thinner and lighter and more brittle than its more massive counterpart. It is, however, moderately tractible and some successful domestication was achieved in the former Belgian Congo. But the bush African elephant is different altogether. Considerably larger—up to 11 feet at the shoulder—its ears are angular and not as rounded as those of the forest elephant, its tusks are broader, more curved and heavier. It is a wholly intractable beast, unpredictable and unmanageable.

The legendary Jumbo is the prime example. He was a massive beast 10 ft 10 ins tall and weighing over six tons. But when he was finally bought by the American showman Phineas T. Barnum it was with considerable relief to the London Zoo authorities who still owned him, for Jumbo was becoming moody and unpredictable. The commercial fact that differentiates the Indian from the African elephant is that in the Indian only the male possesses tusks (the females occasionally carry very short tusks which are referred to as 'tushes' but are generally free of ivory). In the African breeds, however, both sexes carry tusks, and those of the cow elephant are of better quality ivory than those of the male. This simple biological fact has caused probably one of the world's greatest accumulations of human misery and animal exploitation.

Since earliest times ivory has been looked on as a gem. It is easy to carve—for fresh ivory is quite soft. At first it is yellowish in colour due to a high oil content, but this soon dries to white, although in time ivory

African natives used many methods to kill elephants. The weighted spear (J. Bland-Sutton 1811).

fades to a dark brown. The finest ivory is translucent, the worst, mammoth ivory, for the most part collected from the immense mammoth deposits in Siberia, is brittle and cracks easily. But ivory, be it elephant or mammoth or from those other ivory producers, the walrus and the narwhal, has always been valuable. Solomon received ships from Tarshish bearing gold and silver, apes and ivory. Ebony and ivory travelled down the waters of the Nile in the days of the Pharaohs. The ancient Hebrews trafficked in ivory with Assyria. It was used as ransom and tribute. The Phoenicians were skilled carvers of ivory. The Chinese have been the ivory carvers supreme of the ancient and modern worlds in a craft going back at least 6,000 years.

Such a commodity was so valuable that none could be wasted. In the last century the solid tip of each tusk was used for billiard balls, the hollow centre portion for bangles; the ivory dust was assiduously collected and either made into fertilizer, boiled down and used as gelatine, employed as a human tonic, or converted into ivory black as a basis for ink.

The consumption of ivory since ancient times has been immense and has cut heavily into the native populations of the elephant. As long ago as AD 77 Pliny commented 'large elephant teeth in fact are now rarely found except in India, the demands of luxury having exhausted all those in our part of the world.'

Ironically, when the great animal was killed by native Africans, every piece of it was used—except for the ivory. That was piled behind the houses of the chiefs, or left in the forest. The tusks were looked on as no more than slightly different bones, they possessed a certain inherent

The spear attack

beauty and sheen and, shining white, were used to encircle the graves of chiefs. Cattle pens and stockades were made of the great curving tusks, or door posts and pillars, struts and supports for their simple houses. But on the whole it was considered the least useful part and over the decades and centuries tusks accumulated in ever growing heaps, rotting, eaten by rats and abandoned in the heart of Africa.

But since time immemorial the African had killed the elephant for meat. Rock carvings show elephants stuck like pincushions with the spears of natives. Other ancient drawings show them caught in traps or staked pitfalls; techniques varied. The simple attack with the spear was the most straightforward, and elephant spears with huge razor sharp heads were used by many tribes. A variant was to attack from behind, and a well-directed spear could sever the spinal column or even disembowel. Arrows or spearheads dipped in poison were used in many parts of Africa. Some peoples sought to hamstring the animal. This entailed creeping up behind an unsuspecting elephant—which meant in practice one away from the herd—and either severing the massive tendons of the hind leg with an axe, or else—in a true test of manhood—a member of the tribe would rush forward, jump on the rear leg of the chosen elephant where the questing trunk could not reach him and saw away mightily with a knife, until either the tendon was cut through or the enraged creature had rubbed himself free of his assailant on a tree, bush or rock.

Simple or ingenious and of varying efficiency, this killing was on a minute scale. Elephant meat was occasionally dried and kept, but more often it was eaten fresh and when the gorge was over there was little left

Hamstringing

Pitfalls and bows and arrows (Peter Kolb 1719).

except scraps for scavengers and vultures. Killing was strictly for food, and never for killing's sake. And this was a way of life which was to exist for centuries until events of the utmost significance in the emergence and discovery of the continent of Africa began to take place.

Europeans were late on the scene. By the time the early Dutch and Portuguese seamen, traders and explorers started to appear, another nation had been doing business with the Africans for centuries—the Arabs. As early as the ninth century, imports of African ivory were finding their way to Canton in China. When Marco Polo ventured into Asia he heard of what is believed to have been Zanzibar, where the 'teeth' of elephant abounded and, incidentally, where the women were said to be the 'most ill-favoured in the world.' By the thirteenth century Zanzibar was a thriving old-established Arab port. The Arabs hardly ventured inland, they had little need, for the Africans brought their produce to them: gold, copper and above all their ivory. So well established were they that when the Portuguese, the first European nation to venture so far, found their way in easy stages coast-hopping down the west of Africa (coming on the ivory wealth of the Gulf of Guinea and the Ivory Coast itself on their travels) so around the Cape of Good Hope and then up the eastern side of the continent, they were unable to oust them despite a war fought intermittently for close on 100 years.

Soon the Arabs were in control of the whole East African coast,

An elephant hunt in India c. 1813

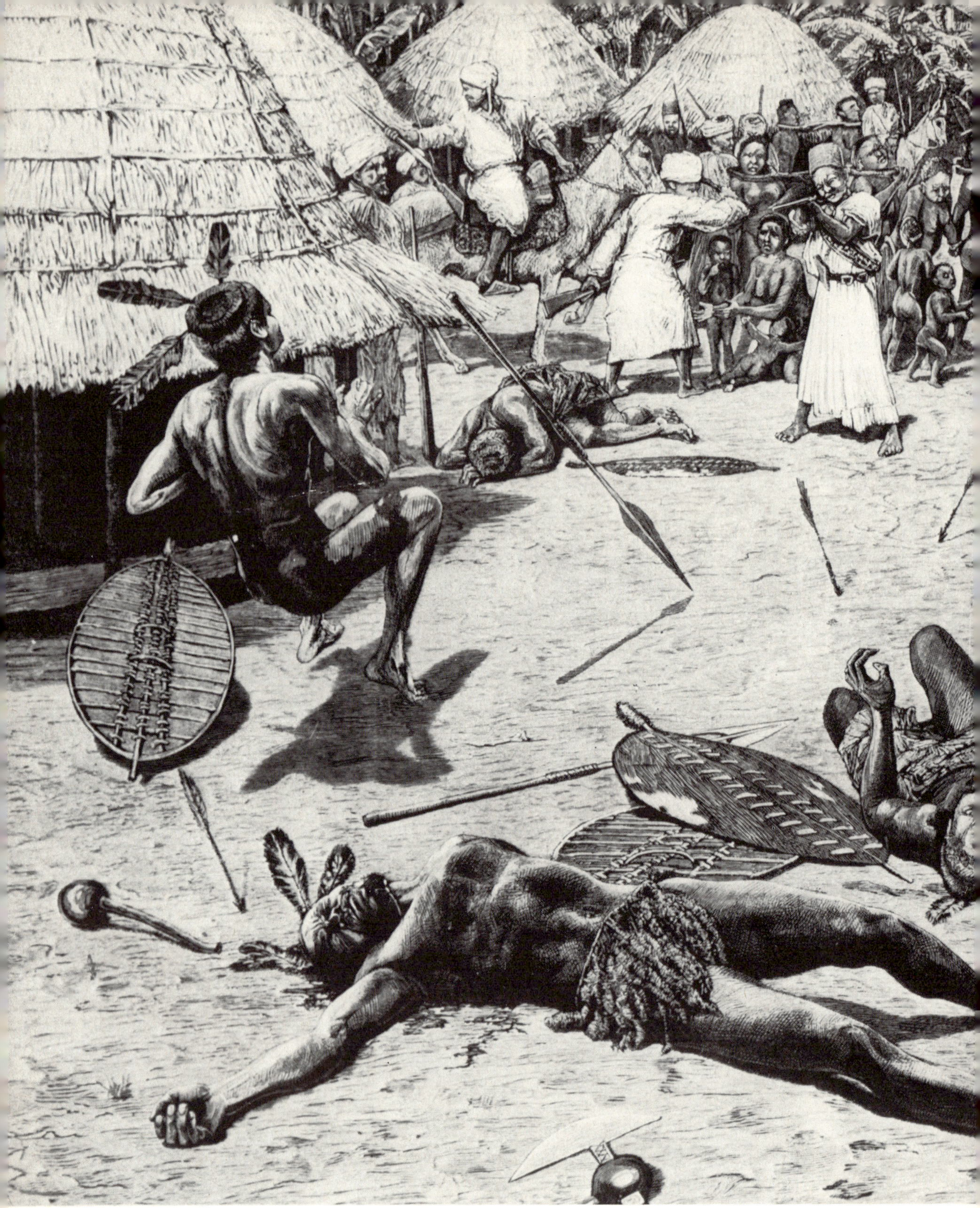

91

(Previous pages) The Arab exploitation of the twin trades of black and white gold left a trail of death and devastation in many parts of Africa.

trading in slaves as well as in ivory. Gradually they began to push inland along the traditional entries into the African interior. Up the Zambezi; from Mombasa through what we know as Kenya into Uganda; from Dar-es-Salaam and penetrating into Tanzania. Theirs was a peaceful entry. They established trading posts on the principal routes, built small communities, planted the seeds which they carried with them, set up their harems and lived in harmony with the local tribesmen. It was an existence of mutual benefit. The Arabs were in the centre of their trading areas, could control the flow of goods to the coast, chiefly ivory, and could live a life of leisure, relaxation and considerable profit; to the African the Arabs offered valuable goods in exchange for the previously worthless 'teeth' which he could collect, with the minimum of effort, from the useless heaps accumulated for so long. Transport for the tusks was more difficult, but there was a seemingly limitless supply of human carriers. For the most part the two nations lived in harmony; when they clashed, as neither possessed firearms, they were evenly matched.

For centuries the traditional markets in the Far East consumed any ivory coming from Africa, and asked for more. But in the early 1800s an explosion of demand from rich European nations set off a chain of events which was to erupt into one of the bloodiest eras in African history.

For the coming of Europeans into the ivory trade also brought guns. No longer need the Arabs negotiate with the tribal chiefs, now they could demand what they wanted and if necessary take it by force. Guns bought power, and as the stocks of tusks diminished in the nearer reaches of Africa and the Arabs were forced to penetrate deeper and deeper into the vast continent they needed protection. The European traders were only too happy to trade tusks for firearms. Zanzibar became an arsenal. Muskets from Germany, more from France, antiquated 'Brown Bess' weapons from British India, blasting powder from the United States, and later rifles. What could be more satisfactory than to combine the twin trades of black and white gold?

The first Europeans to witness this rape of Africa were the early explorers. In 1858 Burton and Speke discovered Lake Tanganyika by following well-worn Arab ivory trails opened 30 years before. During Livingstone's last journey which started in 1866, Tippoo Tip, the greatest of Arab slave and ivory traders, had heard that a solitary white man was wandering in the vicinity and so sent parties to look for him— in case the stranger be taken for one of his own rapacious henchmen. With the greatest of courtesy Tippoo Tip then accompanied Livingstone on his way to discover the great lakes of Mweru and Bangweulu in Zambia.

The Arab approach to the interloping European trespassing on his hunting ground was courteous and helpful. On many occasions exploring party and slave traders banded together for mutual protection. The perfumed elegance of the Arab in their small communities contrasted horrifically with the brutalities of the slaving trade which they conducted without compunction or mercy. The diaries of the explorers are full of chance and prolonged meetings with slave chains, bearing precious ivory on their heads and making their way, in abject misery, to the coast and the auction house, and to a life of subjugation.

The passage of slave traders left swathes of misery across Central Africa and Stanley reported with disgust of coming on one such foray where he saw 2,300 slaves, all women and children, sitting in chained rows with 2,000 tusks beside them and learned with amazed horror that five previous expeditions in the same area had been as 'successful'.

It is difficult to determine when the mountains of old ivory started to run out. But there was no real threat to the living herds as long as the African was only armed with bows and arrows. Arab guns were rarely turned on elephants, they were reserved for human targets, and elephant hunting was considered far too dangerous for the Arabs to indulge in themselves. But when the tribesmen too began to be armed

The professional ivory hunter found a bonanza awaiting him.

Mammoth ivory from Siberian deposits found its way on to the market. Although brittle and variable, it was still good ivory.

with guns and saw the insatiable appetite of the ivory traders for tusks they started to turn their attention in earnest to elephant killing on the grand scale. Had the African elephant been blessed like its Asian cousin with tuskless females, the depredations might have had less effect, but in Africa the female not only carried ivory, it carried the most desirable ivory, as the African was quick to discover. The fight for fresh ivory was on.

And not only for the coast trade of Eastern Africa. In Western Africa, where the Portuguese had been only the first European nation to discover the ivory riches of the region, indiscriminate elephant killing commenced on an incredible scale. As the years passed so tusk weight fell dramatically, showing how disastrous and probably irreversible were the effects on elephant stocks. The average weight of tusks from Gabon, the Cameroons and the Ivory Coast fell from 60 to 20 lbs. The French even laid down a minimum weight below which it was not permitted to trade. They had intended this to be ten pounds, but against the representation of the ivory traders that there was a breed of pygmy elephants (a longstanding belief which has never been either proved or disproved) whose tusks could never attain that weight, they lowered the acceptable minimum to $4\frac{1}{2}$ lbs. This meant that immature elephants were being slaughtered as well.

Far to the south the first white hunters had entered the stage, following on the footsteps of the Dutch settlers who had colonized around the Cape of Good Hope and then trekked north: men like Gordon Cumming, Oswell and Cornwallis Harris, who carved their names in ivory. When Gordon Cumming first appeared on the scene the elephant reigned supreme not far from Table Mountain. However callous the conduct of these early hunters in Africa may appear to modern generations, they certainly lacked neither courage or skill. Their early weapons were wholly inadequate against the tough hide—not for several decades were elephant hunters using the muzzle-loading elephant guns firing $\frac{1}{4}$ pound ball shot with a recoil that could knock over an ox. Now mounted on horseback they galloped after their quarry firing shot after shot at the great bulk hoping that either loss of blood or a lucky shot striking some vital spot would bring the great beast down. It was dangerous, but it was also highly successful. Cumming wrote with pride of shooting four elephants and mortally wounding eight others in a single night.

The era of the great white hunter was about to begin. Partly for sport, partly as an escape from the ennui of civilization, partly for profit from ivory and the indefinable love of hunting. With the publication of Gordon Cumming's book, *Five Years of a Hunter's Life in the Far Interior of South Africa*, in 1850, the lure of the trophy hunter, the lure of safari in Africa began—a pursuit which today takes many to Africa to see and photograph the dwindling game herds. Adventure and narrow escapes these early hunters had by the dozen, but could anything forgive the sheer cruelty and callousness shown by Gordon Cumming, who wrote:

> Halting my horse, I fired at the elephant's shoulder, and secured him with a single shot. The ball caught him high on the shoulder blade, rendering him instantly dead lame. The dogs now came up and barked around him, the old fellow limping to a neighbouring tree, he remained stationary, eyeing his pursuers with a resigned and philosophic air.
>
> I resolved to devote a short time to the contemplation of this noble elephant before I should lay him low; accordingly, having off-saddled the horse beneath a shady tree which was to be my quarters for the night and ensuing day, I quickly kindled a fire and put on the kettle, and in a few minutes my coffee was prepared. There I sat in my forest home, coolly sipping my coffee, with one of the finest elephants in Africa awaiting my pleasure beside a neighbouring tree.
>
> Having admired the elephant a considerable time, I resolved to make experiments for vulnerable points, and, approaching very

near, I fired several bullets at different parts of his enormous skull. These did not seem to affect him in the slightest; he only acknowledged the shots with a 'salaam-like' movement of his trunk, with the point of which he gently touched the wound with a striking and peculiar action... Large tears now trickled from his eyes, which he slowly shut and opened; his colossal frame quivered convulsively, and falling on his side, he expired.

Over the next 20 years the elephant in southern Africa was systematically wiped out and by 1870 the herds which Gordon Cumming had found in such profusion near the Cape were no more. Remorselessly, Boer and other white hunters pressed northward into Rhodesia and Mozambique. Their activities made considerable inroads into the indigenous elephant population, but this was far less than that caused by the native African tribesmen when they came to be armed with guns. A steady plunder of tusks, sent to the coast by ox-cart, coach and, latterly, by rail, marked the passage of the hunters through Africa.

It is difficult to calculate the quantity of ivory, or of slaves, that left

Tusks on the London market, graded according to size and quality.

Elephant feet make fine footstools! Wildlife souvenirs on sale in Kenya before the ban on animal products.

Africa during those decades of the last century. Customs receipts then were as inaccurate and unreliable as they are today. Smuggling was carried on up and down the immense coast of East Africa where an Arab dhow could beach for a few hours, load with white or black cargo and be away on the high seas in a matter of hours. Figures emerge from time to time and even given the fact that they are only a microcosm of the total trade being carried on in the two main commodities, they make startling reading. At Suakin, near the present Port Sudan on the Red Sea—an outlet of importance yet not comparable with Zanzibar, Mombasa or Dar-es-Salaam—a staggering one million elephant tusks passed through the place between 1853 and 1878. Many of these would have been old tusks, but a great many would not.

The breaking of the Arab power in East Africa was a long and bloody struggle. Through a combination of anti-slave trade regulations, now enforced by naval power off the eastern coast, and the colonizing of Africa, by the Belgians and the French from the west, the Germans in Tanganyika through Dar-es-Salaam and the British from several directions, by 1893 the Arab reign was over. By then almost all the tusks to appear on the market were from freshly killed elephants and a noted game hunter of the period wrote, 'The only thing of value the interior of Africa produces at present in any quantity is ivory. . . . The elephant has done much for Africa. The best he can do now for his country is to disappear . . .' The new colonies were faced with a dilemma, for the only produce they could supply was ivory and thus the only way they could be made to pay their way was with ivory.

The great kills began around 1895 and continued for ten years until

From the product of this one killing these men can earn more than they can in an entire year by legal means. Ivory poachers in East Africa.

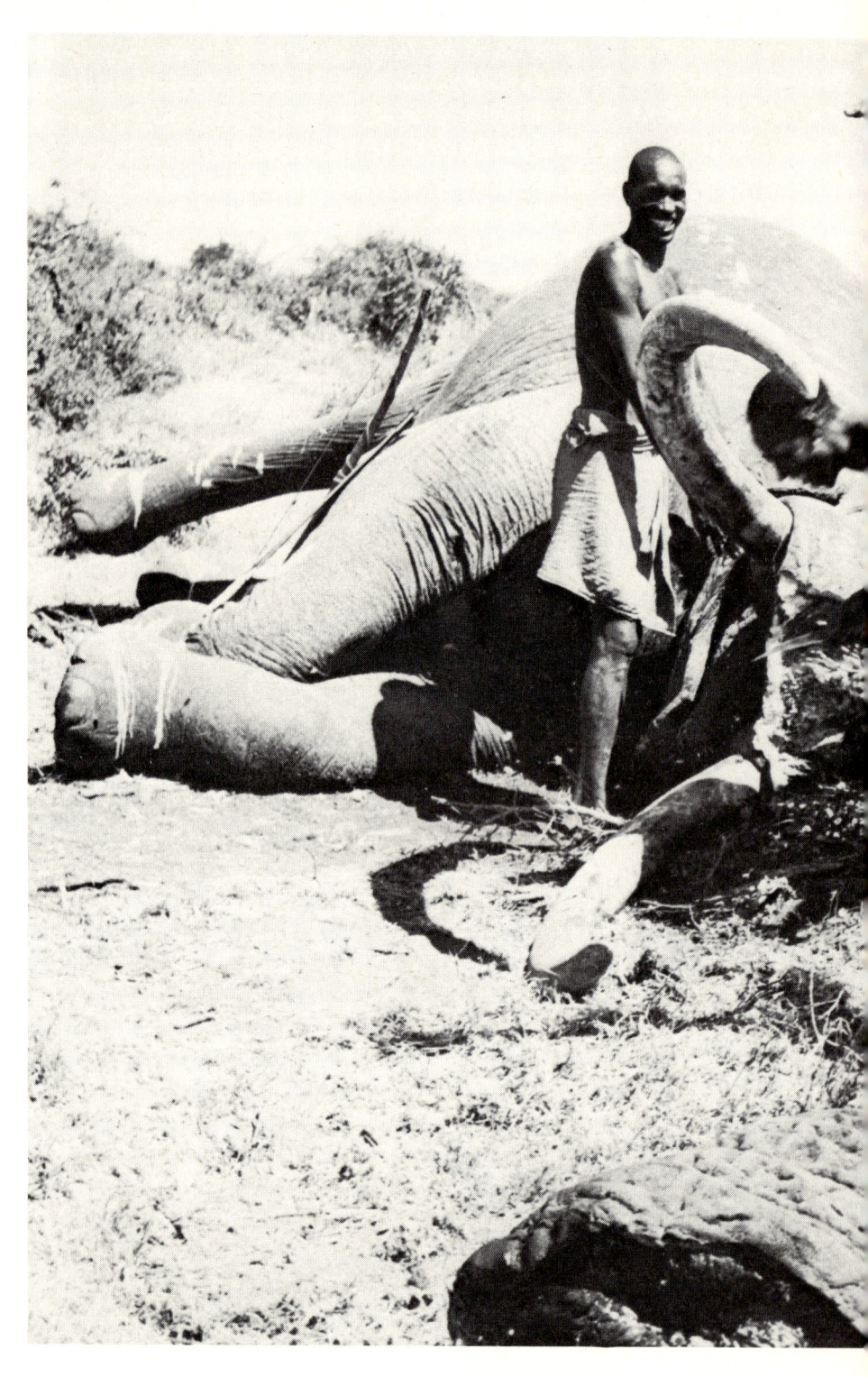

99

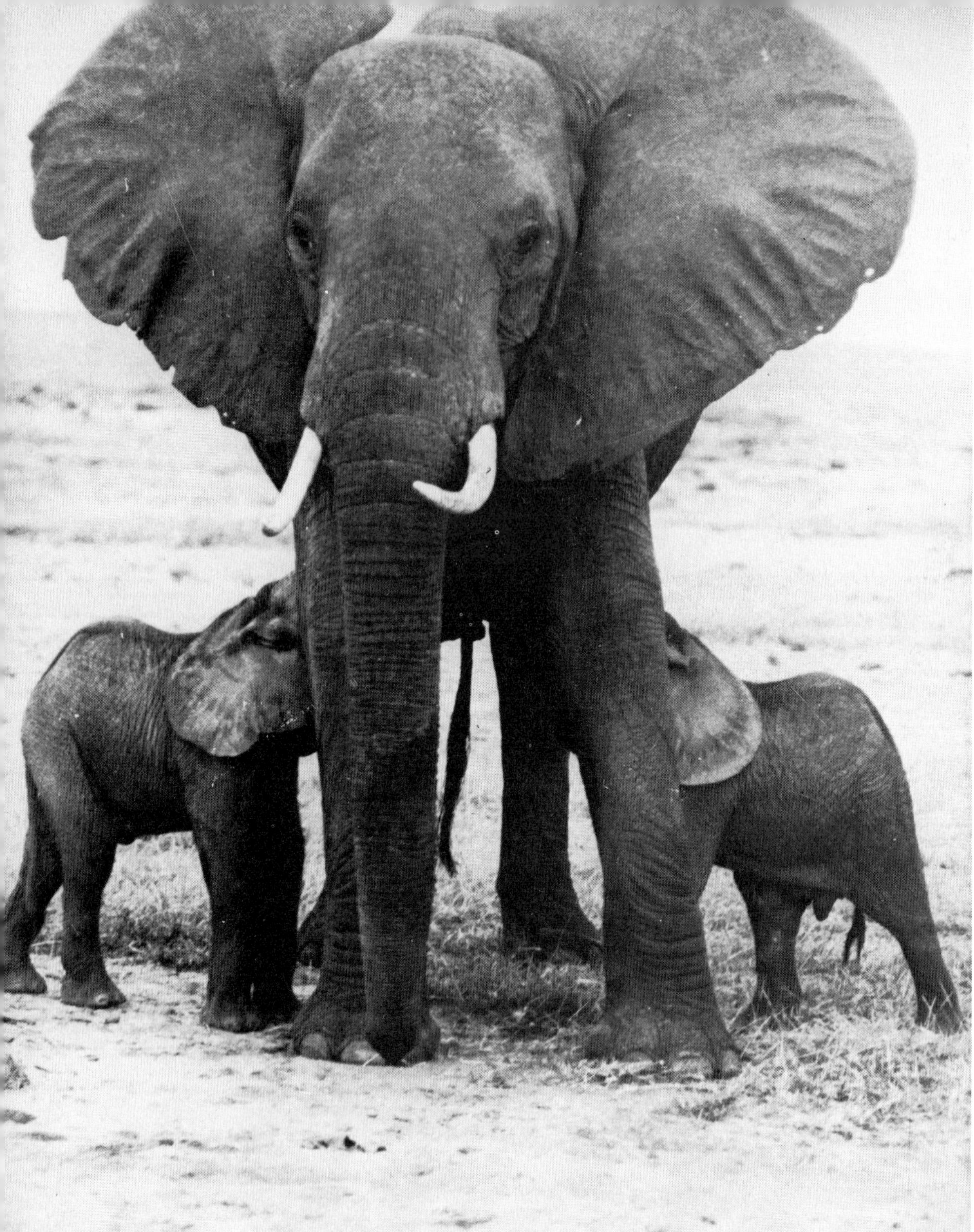

game regulations at last began to take effect. Game laws had been instituted in German East Africa in 1896 and the British followed suit in 'British East' a year later. But it was easier to impose laws than to supervize them. Many hunters stretched the regulations, if they did not wholly ignore them, and the ravages of poacher or hunter went unchecked and unnoticed in that vast country with rudimentary communications.

The principal markets for the ivory accumulated in those years remained the Far East (as indeed it is today for both legal and illicit ivory) but the European demand for combs and hairbrushes, billiard balls, piano keys, chess sets and a host of other ornaments and articles of everyday use also absorbed huge quantities.

The inception of the Kenya railway and that from Dar-es-Salaam brought the hinterland within reach, and it was found that Africa had a great many other things to offer. Ivory became less important to the economies of the emerging colonies, licence fees were imposed and enforced, a complete ban on the shooting of cow elephants was brought into effect and the decline in stocks was slowed.

Today poaching, particularly of the elephant and the black rhino, which is desirable for its horn, continues on a large scale, sometimes even with the active help of game wardens themselves (and who is to blame them when their own wages are so low, and riches are to be had for the picking or the turn of a blind eye). There is uncertainty as to the present population of elephants left in Africa, although the figure is believed to be in the order of 1.2 million. But what is quite clear though is that in certain areas the elephant has declined sharply in recent years. A population of 150,000 elephant in Kenya in 1973 is now thought to be less than half that number. The African elephant appears to have disappeared for good from the Gambia, Guinea-Bissau, Lesotho and Swaziland. Elsewhere numbers are being whittled away. Some of this decline is due to ivory poaching (it is reckoned that the ivory of more than 100,000 elephants left Africa in 1976, principally to the Far East and Hong Kong), human expansion and enlarging agricultural and forest holdings is responsible for more, while confining the wide-ranging elephant in an area too small for him is having a longer-term effect as it eats down its own habitat. But of course, the final death-knell could be political. If southern Africa dissolves into total war it would be naive to imagine that the elephant can be protected in the face of such carnage.

(Opposite) What does their future hold?

'The Lost Glories of an Abundant Land':

The whole with its glittering undulations, marked a space on the face of the heavens resembling the windings of a vast majestic river. When this bend became very great, the birds, as if sensible of the unnecessary circuitous course they were taking, suddenly changed their direction so that what was in column before became an immense front, straightening all its indentures, until it swept the heavens in one vast and infinitely extended line.

    Alexander Wilson, *American Ornithology*, 1808–1814

Disappearing Birds

One cannot estimate the number of passenger pigeons in the United States in Wilson's time. It is believed that they could have been counted, if such counting were possible, in the several thousand million—a figure nearing half the entire bird population of the United States at that time.

The passenger pigeon, a handsome bird, was some 16 inches long with a black bill and glittering fiery orange eye. Overall blue-grey on wings and back, the throat, breast and flanks were of a rich reddish hazel colour, and the lower part of the neck either gold, green or purplish crimson. Chief Pokagon of the Michigan Indians, who was to witness the elimination of almost the last colony of the passenger pigeon said, 'It was proverbial with our fathers that if the Great Spirit in his wisdom could have created a more elegant bird in plumage, form and movement, he never did.' If singly the passenger pigeon was a beautiful bird, in the vast masses in which it was always seen it created an indelible impression on those who observed it. The distinguished ornithologist and artist, John James Audubon, wrote:

> Gliding through the woods and close to the observer, it passes like a thought, and on trying to see it again, the eye searches in vain, the bird is gone ... I cannot describe to you the extreme beauty of their aerial evolutions, when a hawk chanced to press upon the rear of the flock. At once, like a torrent, and with a noise like thunder ... they darted forward in undulating and angular lines, descended and swept close over the earth with inconceivable velocity, mounted perpendicularly so as to resemble a vast column, and, when high, were seen wheeling and twisting within their continued lines, which then resembled the coils of a gigantic serpent.

The passage of such a prodigious number of birds could only be marked in time.

The passenger pigeon, though, had a fatal weakness—it was good to eat. The dark meat of the older adult birds was inclined to be tough, but the younger ones were tender and sweet and delicious, eaten either fresh or smoked. And when humans were satiated by a steady diet of pigeon, the farmers found a cheap and apparently endless source of food for their hogs. The Indians, as well as eating the bird, used the fat as a substitute for butter and as the bird was so useful they practised a form of game conservation by leaving the adult birds alone while the young were still dependent upon them. The white man had no such inhibitions.

In flight the birds were packed so tight that a single shot could, and often did, bring down up to one dozen birds. Where the flock passed over a low hill, people on the ground could knock them down with long poles. In New England in particular, the predeliction of the bird for salt led to artificial salt beds being laid and then netted. When enough birds had

(Opposite) The passenger pigeon or Ectopistes migratorius.

'At once, like a torrent, and with a noise like thunder . . .' One of the mighty flocks of passenger pigeons passing over waiting gunners.

gathered for the feast the nets were sprung. A keen rivalry sprang up between the netters who sought quiet and the shooters who fired at every pigeon they could find—the only losers were the pigeons.

The pigeon nested in the northern woods and forests and with the approach of winter flew to warmer climes. Its diet was of beech nuts, acorns and chestnuts, but it had fairly catholic taste and could strip an area with astonishing speed. So rapacious were these invasions that on more than one occasion the Bishop of Montreal went to the lengths of excommunicating the entire breed—with surprisingly little effect.

At the roosting sites would be men armed with guns, clubs, long poles and pots of sulphur to blind and confuse the birds. As the pigeons came in their wings made a roar like thunder. The noise was terrific and terrified the horses while overhead, swinging in lazy circles, were hawks, buzzards and eagles awaiting their pick. At nightfall the gunners would move about the woods firing in volleys at the massed birds above them. Sometimes 50 or more would fall at a time and be collected, while countless more were wounded and crept away into the undergrowth to perish. It was not uncommon for a party of three guns to end with a bag of over 5,000 birds, as evidence of a single night's work.

Audubon wrote of one such evening,

Few pigeons were then to be seen, but a great number of persons, with horses and wagons, guns and ammunition had already established encampments on the borders ... Suddenly there burst forth a general cry of 'Here they come!' The noise which they made, though yet distant, reminded me of a hard gale at sea through the rigging of a close-reefed vessel ... As the birds arrived and passed over me, I felt a current of air that surprised me ... The pigeons arriving by thousands, alighted everywhere, one above another, until solid masses as large as hogsheads were formed on the branches all around. Here and there the perches gave way under the weight with a crash ... It was a scene of uproar and confusion. Even the reports of the guns were seldom heard ... Towards the approach of day the authors of this devastation began their entry amongst the dead, the dying and the mangled. The pigeons were picked up and piled in heaps until each had as many as he could possibly dispose of.

Then the farmers' hogs, which had been driven nearby, were turned loose to fatten on the remaining carcases.

The mass of birds could strip an area like a whirlwind —but when they came to feed the netters would be lying in wait.

It was at the nesting sites, though, that the greatest slaughter could be effected. By the 1880s the telegraph system was in full and efficient operation. The local railroad superintendents, who stood to profit when the catch went to market were warned to be on the lookout for the nesting sites. As a result the same flock might be reported from upwards of 20 different places. It was then a question of calculating where would be enough food to sustain the huge mass of breeding birds. When that was narrowed down and the site detected, the professional pigeon killers assembled together with local farmers, hunters and every able-bodied man, woman and child in the district—a small army up to 3,000 strong at times.

When the birds had congregated and the squabs were at their fattest, yet could not fly, the pigeon gatherers moved in. Sometimes fires were lit around the woods and the bewildered birds were beaten down with rakes, sticks and spades. Others were netted and packed live in their thousands for use in the trap shooting contests which were a principal diversion in the United States at that time. The dead birds were then packed in ice and sent to the cities of the east.

The nesting sites in the northern forests were of a colossal size. One was found to cover an area three miles wide by 30 miles long and within this every tree was packed with nests, sometimes 100 or more to a tree. In this one site it was estimated that there were an incredible 30 to 50 million birds, and it was by no means the largest. The noise of the chattering birds, which had a shrill, raucous cry, was indescribable and could be heard miles away. And when the birds finally left the site after the young had fledged, the place was left as barren as though a tornado had passed. The trees were stripped of their leaves. Many branches and boughs had snapped under the sheer weight of nesting birds and a number of trees were killed 'as completely as if girdled by an axe'. The ground beneath was several inches deep with droppings, the smell was almost unbearable and it took years for the landscape to recover.

With evidence of so many millions of birds it was not surprising that Audubon declared that:

> The passenger pigeon needs no protection. Wonderfully prolific and having vast forests of the north as its breeding grounds, traveling hundreds of miles in search of food, it is here today and elsewhere tomorrow, and no ordinary destruction can lessen them or be missed from the myriads that are yearly produced.

Yet when that was written the passenger pigeon was already becoming less numerous in certain parts of the eastern United States. The decline was attributed, ironically, to the wayward habits of the birds; others may have supported an Indian's comment 'Pigeon heap damned fool, fly in Big Water, no come back'. But the truth was that the wholesale netting of the birds in New England was already making drastic inroads into the population. Also the formidable loss of forest as settlement spread across the United States materially aided the birds' ultimate extinction, but the prime cause of its demise was slaughter on a staggering scale.

Between 1867 and 1877 an average of over 10,000,000 birds a year were taken from the flocks in the Middle West. In 1878 an entire colony was wiped out in an orgy of killing which led to five freight cars a day heading to market bearing the spoils—and this continued for 30 days on end. The few survivors of this flock with many others went to Manitoba where a late winter saw the death of thousands more.

When the birds became scarce in one locality, it was thought, naively, they had gone elsewhere. Some states tried to restrict the slaughter, and laws were passed prohibiting the use of gun or net within one mile of a nesting site. But these were ignored or conveniently forgotten and in most cases were unenforceable. The 1880s saw the introduction in common use of the breech-loader and this was responsible for more efficient killing. In 1881 in one area alone 500 men took an average of 20,000 birds each. Many of these hunters were newly arrived immigrants, and with no other means of subsistence they turned pigeon hunter, shooting and trapping for market—one netter took 6,000 birds in a single day. Most states, however, had no close season for migratory birds, so the slaughter could go on unchecked. That on the breeding grounds around Lake Superior eventually proved decisive. The final stand of the passenger pigeon was in northern Michigan.

A number of specimens of this attractive bird had been taken into captivity. But they would not breed satisfactorily—perhaps they needed to be surrounded by a throng of thousands before they could feel at home—and eventually, incredibly, only a single bird remained of the millions of the remarkable passenger pigeon which had once graced American skies. Martha, as she was affectionately called, died in September 1914, in the Cincinnatti Zoological Gardens, the same year that another attractive but highly destructive American bird, the Carolina Parakeet, vanished into extinction. Of the passenger pigeon a bird lover wrote, 'I regret their departure. To me they were one of the lost glories of an abundant land.' In our war to dominate the natural world there has never been a battle of such staggering annihilation of a bird species as that of the passenger pigeon.

Those birds restricted to islands where faced with no natural predators they have lost their power of flight, were to prove particularly vulnerable. So it was in New Zealand. Here bred a number of races of flightless birds, from the strange kiwi (pronounced 'impossible' by British naturalists when the first one came to Europe in 1813) standing no more than 18 inches high, to the giant moas. Twenty-four extinct species of moa in five different genera have been identified. Some were smaller than turkeys, others about the size of the ostrich, but the giant of the family was *Dinornis maximus*, a towering 12 foot tall. Some of the moas had been extinct for

The moa (extinct) and the kiwi—two of the flightless birds indigenous to New Zealand (from an old print).

many centuries, but some were certainly alive at the time of the Maori voyages from the Polynesian islands to settle in New Zealand less than 1,000 years ago. Undisturbed for centuries in a land where there were no birds of prey and no rodents, the moas soon fell easy victims to the Maori hunters who sought their flesh and eggs. It is believed that the moa may indeed have provided an important means of sustenance for the Maori, and with their disappearance anthropologists feel that there was no recourse but to turn to the cannibalism which so shocked early European settlers.

An interesting aftermath to the story took place in 1948 when another flightless bird, the New Zealand takahe, was found on South Island. The takahe was believed extinct since 1898 when, 50 years later, the strange footprints of a bird were seen in the soft mud by a lakeside. Extensive search unearthed the bird, and it is thought that the colony, now under the strictest protection, may number over 100 pairs.

Flightless too were a number of birds to be found only on a group of

The dodo. A portrait by Roelandt Savery of one of the captive birds that was brought to Europe.

islands known as the Mascarenes in the middle of the Indian Ocean, of which Mauritius is the best known.

For centuries Arab traders pursuing their commerce with Africa had passed and occasionally visited the Mascarenes. But the islands seemed to have little to offer, so having replenished with food and water there was no need to linger. Early Portuguese navigators too found the Mascarenes and one, Pedro Mascarenhas, gave his name to the group of three islands, the only break in the monotonous expanse of the Indian Ocean. But it was left to a Dutchman, Jacob Corneliszoon van Neck to make the first mention of a creature that came to be called the dodo, and to bring back the bird to Europe.

The lesser dodo or Didunculus.

The Dutch called these strange creatures *walghvogels* (nauseous birds) as they were disgusting to eat, but they were like no other birds the Dutchman had ever set eyes upon. 'Larger than our swans,' van Neck described them, 'with huge heads only half covered with skin, as if clothed with a hood.' 'Great Fowles' an Englishman with van Neck called them, 'having great heads and upon their heads a skin, as if they had caps on their heads, they have no wings at all, but in place of wings, they have four or five small curled feathers, and their colour is grayish.'

The dodo was a huge ungainly bird, so clumsy that it could barely waddle on its short legs and spindly broad feet. In colour it was ash-grey, with yellowish, whitish wings. Its huge head carried a fiercesome black beak with a pronounced hook. It possessed no natural enemies and had long since lost the power of flight or even of moving quickly for it had no need, until man came to disturb its peace. It nested on the ground in little hollows, so it was vulnerable during all its natural existence. Tame, bewildered, comical and very stupid, the dodo 'sate still', recorded the same Englishman in his diary, 'and could not flie down from us, so thatt we with our handes might easily take them.'

If van Neck's crew had found the dodo disgusting to eat, some of his successors were not so fastidious and would load their ships with salted *walghvogel* for the long voyage to the Indies.

So convenient were the Mascarenes that the Dutch soon established a colony there and with the colonists came dogs, and pigs, and above all rats. They soon found that the eggs and chicks of the slow-moving, dim-witted dodo made excellent eating when young so the settlers killed and salted the birds and sold them to passing ships. An English traveller in 1634 called at Mauritius and reported seeing a quantity of dodo; when he returned four years later there were none left and he sorrowfully recalled, 'they were as bigge bodied as great Turkeyes, covered with Downe, having little hanguing wings like shortt sleeves, altogether unuseffull to Fly withal, or any way with them to helpe themselves.'

In 1681 it is believed that the last dodo was killed on Mauritius, and around the same time similar dodo-like relatives, native to the other islands of the Mascarenes, Reunion and Rodriguez, also became extinct. The only relic of the dodo was a single moth-eaten specimen in the Ashmolean Museum at Oxford—and so bedraggled was this that in 1755 the decision was made to burn it. Some enthusiast kept the head and a foot which are still at Oxford. And that is almost all that is left of the dodo, apart from a number of drawings taken from life from the few birds that reached Europe alive.

Of the 'Bignes of a Goose, a coal black Head and back, with a white Belly and a Milk white Spot under one of their Eyes, which Nature has ordered to be under the right Eye,' is how the great auk is described in an early navigational journal. It lived in a 'land of constant Fog, especially from the Month of May to the Month of July and most part of

August, which is the time that all Ships bound to this Country, do generally come, and therefore ought to keep a very good look out lest they be deceived.'

The fisherman's larder. The great auk, a bird once common in the Arctic.

Early mariners and fishermen who explored and worked in the inhospitable waters of the North Atlantic knew the great auk well. In times past the bird had frequented much of the Atlantic coast to as far south as Spain for fossils of the great auk have even been found in Italy and elsewhere in the Mediterranean, and across the Atlantic as far south as Florida. But in general it preferred colder waters.

Here the Vikings had hunted it with avidity, and when the cold north regions became known to the seafarers of the sixteenth century here they found the great auk, or garefowl, in profusion. Starved of fresh meat, to the seamen discovering the bird on its nesting site this was a heaven-sent gift. In the water it could outswim the fastest rowing boat, but on land it could barely walk, let alone run from danger. Eaten fresh they were very good, eaten salted they were none too bad and their eggs were considered the greatest delicacy. To hungry fishermen the great auk larder seemed unending. Soon the bird became the staple diet of the fishing fleets of many nations. Little of the bird was wasted as the feathers were kept to stuff beds and pillows—and this became a substantial trade in later years. Auk fat fed their fires. A dried auk made an excellent torch, so rich was it in fat. The bones were used as fishhooks or needles. With some justification a seafarer of those days wrote, 'God made the innocencie of so poor a creature to become such an admirable instrument for the sustentation of man.'

By 1829 the great auk was confined to one inhospitable island off the North Atlantic, and even a colony which had settled on St Kilda, off the west coast of Scotland, was wiped out and it was no longer profitable to carry out large scale expeditions to kill the few survivors.

By 1829 the Great Auk was confined to one inhospitable island off Iceland, Geirfuglasker. Then nature took a turn, a volcanic disturbance destroyed Geirfuglasker and with it what was believed to be the last nesting colony. With the birds' apparent demise museum directors the world over suddenly became aware that they could not number the scarce seabird among their collections. Frantically, expeditions were despatched on the slim chance that somewhere a few stragglers might still exist in the northern seas, and sure enough they found a remnant, on the nearby island of Eldey, of some 50 specimens which had escaped the destruction of Geirfuglasker. Systematically, the last of the great auks were hunted down to satisfy the vanity of the museum curators. In 1844 the last survivor was killed to fulfil the ambitions of an Icelandic bird collector.

The beauty of plumes, cockades and feathered headdresses has delighted man since the earliest days of civilization. The softness and suppleness of feathers, their grace and elegance, the distinction they gave the wearer, their bright and gleaming colours have made the birds they once adorned the prey of man for centuries.

Peacock fans were in wide use in ancient Egypt, and the more beautiful and exotic feathers exchanged hands for prices greater than the rarest jewel. In Greece, ladies sported heron headdresses. In ancient Rome soldiers wore cocks' plumes on their helmets. With the Aztecs of Central America it was the beautiful feathers of the Quetzal that were most highly prized.

Feathers to excite any lady of fashion. 'Le Plumassier' from Diderot's Encyclopédie.

Netting birds.

In Europe the earliest centres of the feather trade were in Italy, in Genoa, Venice and Pisa. Gradually the commerce spread north and by the late seventeenth century in Paris *Les Plumassiers de Panache* were an established industry. Their wares were principally heron and egret feathers, and those of pheasant and the brighter coloured indigenous birds, together with the ostrich which was still being hunted in North Africa. By the latter half of the eighteenth century, plumes and feathers were an accepted part of the society scene and were worn widely on hats and helmets; for the most part these were ostrich plumes.

The fashion grew. By the beginning of the last century the ostrich-plume trade was very big business and firmly established in Paris, London and elsewhere. Ladies of society would consider themselves ill-dressed had they not their enormous ostrich plumes topping their piled hair. Ostrich plumes too were sometimes ousted by those of the egret, and most prized of all were the exotic, almost unbelievably beautiful feathers of the birds of paradise.

Plumes, cockades and feathered headdresses. 'Le Carrousel' from Le Dictionnaire du Théâtre *by Arthur Pugin.*

'Born in paradise'. The bird of paradise being hunted by natives of New Caledonia (from A. R. Wallace's The Malay Archipelago*).*

First brought to Europe in the only surviving vessel of Magellan's circumnavigation, the *Victoria*, in 1522, by 1600 a considerable trade in bird of paradise skins, or rather those of *Paradisea minor* and *Paradisea apoda* was taking place in Europe. The skins were of colours so bright and of a texture so light that they could indeed have been conceived in heaven. They puzzled the scientists of the day for they had no bones and no feet. How could these beautiful birds unlike anything ever seen exist? One distinguished naturalist declared, 'This very beautiful bird, which never sits upon the earth or any other thing is born in paradise.' Another surmised, 'We are of the opinion that these birds live on dew and the nectar of the spice trees. But however that may be, it is quite certain that they never decay,' and then he added, 'They do all their business in flight.' The natives of what is now Papua New Guinea would shoot the mature birds in full plumage with knob-headed arrows so as to stun them and avoid damaging the beautiful plumage, skin them and stretch the skins on a frame where they hardened. Then as the market grew, professional shooters from neighbouring islands added their own considerable haul to the number of skins finding their way to Europe.

Once numerous in Morocco and Algeria, by the middle of the last century the ostrich had been hunted out of great stretches of Africa.

For 50 years from 1820 to 1870 the plumes of heron, egret and bird of paradise, together with those of the ostrich, reigned supreme in the milliner's art in Europe. As the indigenous stocks of ostrich in the Sudan, Arabia, North and South Africa became depleted before the onslaught of the plume hunters, so in the 1860s it was discovered in South Africa that the ostrich could be farmed and that ostrich farming was not only practicable, but profitable. Gradually ostrich farmed feathers came to dominate the market.

As explorers penetrated the hitherto unknown parts of the globe, as communications improved and settlers and immigrants sought profitable lines of business, they came across more and more exotic and beautiful birds. From around 1870 a new world opened for the millinery trade. The search for fancy feathers, *Les Plumes Fantasies* — as the trade called them — became a stampede which over the following half century was to reduce and threaten bird species in a way never before and never since experienced.

Whereas previously it was only the rich who could afford the ostrich plumes that adorned hat and headdress, the now improving standard of living made it possible for others to have them too. And if they could not attain the fashionable extravagance of sprays of egret feathers (which soon, and quite incorrectly, came to be called ospreys) or the wonderful exotic colours of the feathers and skins of the birds of paradise, more humble birds suited their needs and their purses. Not content with a few feathers in a hat, now fashion decreed that entire birds should be seen on what rapidly became an outrageous fashion. Nothing was immune from the milliners' hands. 'Mercury wings' of gulls, swallows, even blackbirds were often to be seen. Entire humming-birds 'hovered'

Bird fans were decorated with stuffed and highly coloured birds.

(Opposite) The macabre passion for stuffed birds.

119

grotesquely over artificial flowers. Owls heads might be seen as though perched on the wearer's head. Small birds in 'earnest incubation' might be found peering from beneath bogus foliage. Dresses were fringed with finches' heads, possibly surrounded by robins' feathers, or edged with swallows' wings. Ribbon bows, each with a skylark's head sown on them were sold as 'chanticleer bows'. Groups of swallows or buntings pursued each other in macabre chase around the crown of a hat.

Millinery art reached a high point around the end of the nineteenth century.

A KILLING HAT.

[" *The dealers declare that the demand for birds of every description will this year be greater than ever.*"—FASHION PAPER.]

(With apologies to the Shade of Shenstone.)

I have found out a gift for my fair—
'Tis a paradise plume for her hat;
   The naturalists think
   The bird's getting extinct:
She will like it the better for that.

I have found out a gift for my fair—
An owl's head to put in her hat;
   There is not a bird
   More useful, I've heard:
But my sweet, she won't mind about that.

I have found out a gift for my fair—
A kingfisher's skin laid out flat;
   It's a bird that don't sing
   And a quite worthless thing
Except to be stuck in a hat.

I have found out a gift for my fair—
Two sea-swallows' wings for her hat;
   Fixed on to the owl
   It does look a queer fowl:
But my love, she won't think about that.

I have found out a gift for my fair—
A white egret's plume for her hat;
   'Twas the honeymoon crest
   Of a bird on its nest:
But she won't care a rap about that.

I have found out a gift for my fair—
A pair of stork legs—think of that!
   If they do look absurd
   That's the fault of the bird,
Not to grow legs more fit for a hat.

            L. G.

As the fashion swept through society, it was said that Ladies

Are not content with looking like a jay,
But they must dress as lightly as a gay;
Nay, ev'ry tail, of ev'ry bird they rob,
And with the lightest feather wing the nob;
Like horses move in the funereal train
Beneath their plumes, and shake the plaited mane.
Now, since to ornament the frolic fair,
There's not one pretty bird whose rump's not bare;
Do not the ladies more or less appear,
Just like the birds whose various plumes they wear.

Louis Octave Uzanne, 'Feathers', *1900*

The great fashion houses of London, Paris, New York, Berlin and Vienna employed teams of hunters to scour the jungles and forests, the swamps and the shores of many lands in the endless search for feathers and bird skins. The plumage trade in Britain and the United States was a thriving and burgeoning commerce. In and around Paris there were alone more than 10,000 people employed in the feather industry. The growth of ladies' journals and fashion magazines showed the latest modes in feathers and what the best-dressed were wearing in the centres of fashion. Those who lived in the provinces need must ape them, and the whole created an almost insatiable market for feathers and bird skins. Singed in acid, trimmed, oxydized, blanched or dyed, stretched, curled, shaped, flattened, mounted or backed, often on silk, the preparation of feathers was an art requiring high skill and finesse. It also required a quite astonishing number of feathers and bird skins.

From the earliest days of the feather boom, voices were raised in protest at the destruction of so much bird life. For the most part this was done on commercial and economic, rather than humanitarian grounds. First, to receive the sanctuary of protection in Britain were the seabirds. On many shores, and particularly beneath Flamborough Head in Yorkshire, the gull shooters were highly active, even on the Thames in London gulls had been shot to the considerable 'affright' of passers-by. Now it was pointed out that the gulls were the farmers' friend as they grubbed up harmful insects, and they were also the sailors' friends as their cries gave warning of approaching land. While to the fishermen they often gave indication of shoals of fish. In 1869 the Seabird Protection Act was passed by the Parliament in London.

The seabirds of Britain were fortunate, for virtually no other bird in the land was safe from the needs of fashion, be they the humble crow or starling, to the crested grebe, swallows, owls or hawks. But it was in the *plumes fantasies* that the real demand lay. This was the 'curse of beauty', as one bird lover exclaimed, for from far and wide and in incredible

(Opposite) 'Born to be slaughtered'. The beautiful dorsal feathers of the egret at breeding time were the most highly sought after. The little egret or Egretta garzetta.

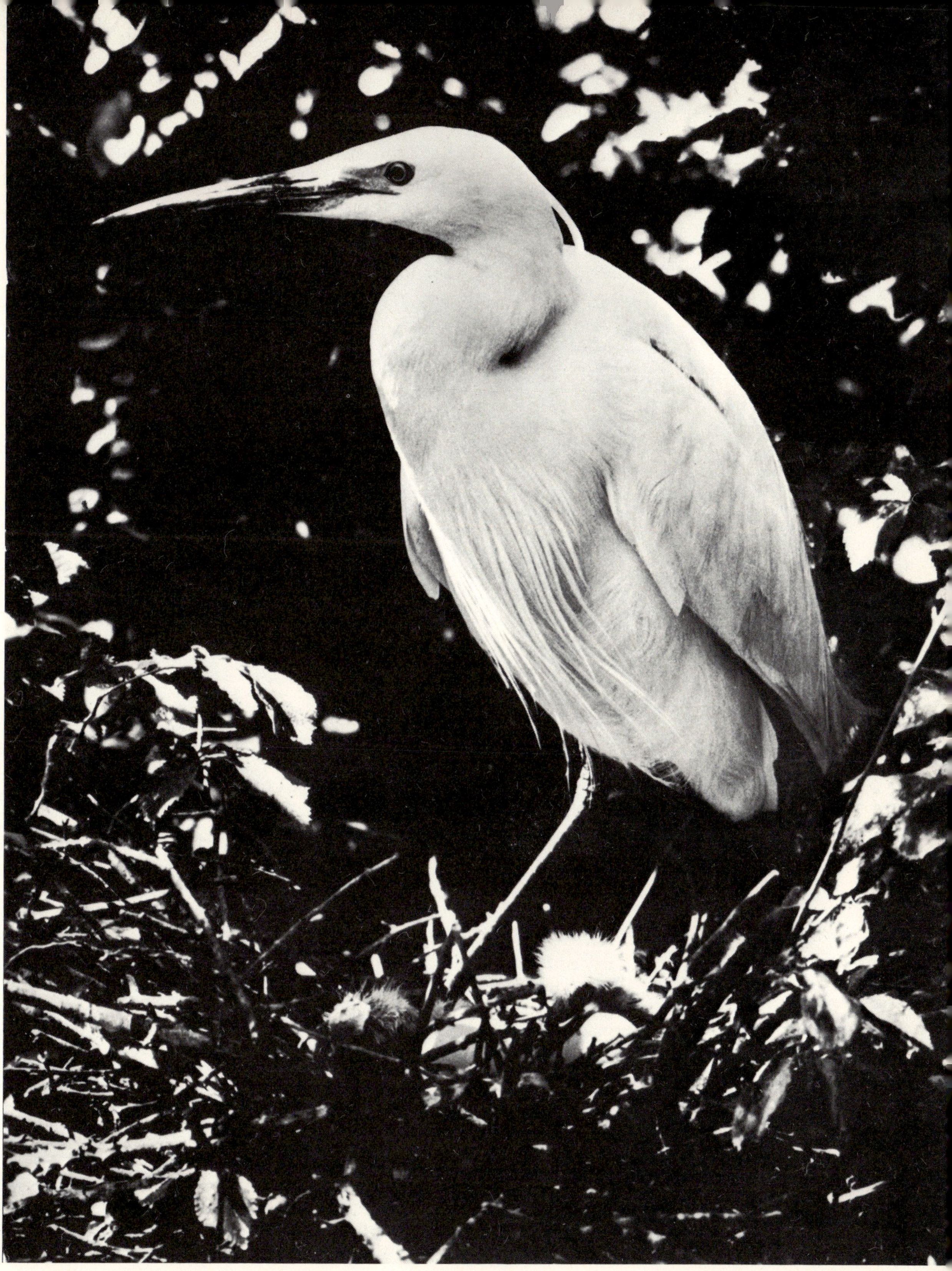

quantities came the truly exotic feathers and skins of a huge variety of birds. Skins of the Himalayan monal pheasant, then called the Impeyan pheasant, from the north of India, vied with the white feathers of the storks. The silver wing coverts of the condor were highly prized. From South America also came the feathers of parrots and whole humming-birds—the little 'flying jewels'. The imperial green tail feathers of the quetzal from Central America were outrageously expensive. India provided, among others, black partridges, blue jays, golden orioles, hoopoes and kingfishers. From Tropical Africa came guineafowl, weaver birds and bronze blackbirds. The lyre-bird and the orange plumes of the golden bower bird were much sought after from Australia. China exported 'osprey' sprays for fan making, and eagle skins. Colder northern regions such as Russia produced the willow-grouse in profusion (in 1900 *ten tons* of wings, for dyeing, found their way on to western markets), they also exported the feathers of gulls, teal and terns, as well as the glossy skins of the black-throated diver for trimmings. And a parallel trade in down for pillows and bolsters kept up a steady demand for eider duck and other sea birds.

Though great was the slaughter of all the beautiful, and many of the not-so-beautiful birds of the world, the prime target was the egret. Most sought-after was *Casmeridius albus*, the great white egret, with a range that covered many parts of both the Old and New Worlds. More numerous were the smaller species, the snowy egret of America (*Egretta thula*), the little egret (*Egretta garzetta*), which was to be found as far afield as southern Europe, through China, Japan, Burma, India, Ceylon, the Malayan archipelago and Africa, and the black-footed egret (*Garzetta nigripes*), with a more restricted range covering Java, the Moluccan Islands and Australia. Other members of the heron family were also coveted, but it was always the beautiful pure white feathers as soft as silk of the other species of egret that were most highly prized.

It was the dorsal plumes of the smaller egrets which stretched the length of the back and could attain a length of ten inches, which were sought by the milliners. But these only attained their full length and full beauty at the time of courtship and nesting. It was almost as though nature had condemned the egret to be slaughtered on its breeding grounds. The lovely white plumes, or *aigrettes*, weighed next to nothing. A full-grown bird would yield $\frac{1}{4}$ ounce of feathers and only $\frac{1}{6}$ ounce of plumes, for very few feathers in the plumage were marketable—the heron could yield three times this quantity and from breast as well as back, but the feathers themselves commanded a fraction of the price of top-grade egret aigrettes which were fetching twice their weight in gold at the turn of this century.

As the egret nested in the highest branches of flimsy trees the only way to get them was to shoot, thus to get the feathers it was necessary to kill the bird. Then the few marketable plumes would be taken from the back of the dead, but often only dying, bird with a small piece of skin still adhering. The carcase would be left for carrion; there was no other use, it was unpalatable. One kilogramme of feathers meant the slaughter of 700 egrets. A single 'lot' in a London auction house in 1900 was the product of the killing of 24,000 egrets. Two years before it was estimated that 1,500,000 egrets were being slaughtered in Venezuela alone.

The most advantageous time for plume collecting was when the young were nearly fledged and the parents were at their most solicitous. Then, when disturbed, the adult birds were most loth to desert the nesting area and were an easy prey for the gunners. The result was a litter of dead adult egrets, their backs torn and bloody where the aigrettes had been cut off, and above in the nests were left abandoned eggs or a pitiful brood of young egrets which had no other fate than to slowly starve to death. An Australian naturalist came on an egret heronry ravaged by the plume hunters:

> What a holocaust! Plundered for their plumes. What a monument of human callousness! There were fifty birds ruthlessly destroyed, besides their young (about 200) left to die of starvation! This last fact was betokened by at least seventy carcases of the nestlings, which had become so weak that their legs had refused to support them and they had fallen from the nests into the water below and had been miserably drowned; whilst in the trees above, the remainder of the parentless young ones could be seen staggering in their nests, some of them falling with a splash into the water as their waning strength left them too exhausted to hold on any longer ... Others again, were seen trying in vain to attract the attention of passing Egrets which were flying with food in their bills to feed their own young, and it was a pitiful sight indeed to see the starvelings with outstretched necks and gaping bills imploring passing birds to feed them.

Such cruelty aroused the wrath of every bird lover. The egret colonies in South America came under the full glare of publicity, and led to duplicity of the lowest order by those vested interests who saw their lucrative feather trade likely to disappear in a storm of revulsion, if the bird societies had their way and popular opinion followed suit.

It was pointed out that the egret scandal was widely exaggerated. That in Venezuela in particular were *garceros*, homes of breeding egrets, and *dormitorios*, where were the unmated birds, and that both these reserves were closely protected. That in the former the feathers, when moulted, were duly gathered and harvested, that there was no killing and no cruelty.

Moulted feathers were indeed collected, they were known as 'dead feathers' and as usually dirty and in poor condition received the lowest price. Whereas 'live feathers' torn from the birds themselves were at the top of the market. 'Murder was endemic' roundly declared a local

United States consul when asked to examine the truths and the half-truths of what went on in the *garceros*. For the egret on the *garceros* and elsewhere was hunted down without mercy; by canoe, for it nested in marsh and forest swamp, by horseback where this was possible, and even to the extent of poisoning the feeding grounds. Wounded egrets would be propped up as decoys for others flying over and they stayed there until they died or were eaten by the virulent red ants.

Systematically, the egret colonies in South America, in Peru, Colombia and Ecuador were wiped out by the plume hunters. Those in Mexico soon went the same way, as did those in Hungary, the Volga Delta and northern Egypt. Whereas formerly the French fashion houses sent their own feather merchants to take the pick of aigrettes, by 1895 it was no longer worth their while.

In the United States a powerful lobby supported the feather merchants, 'I really want to know' asked Senator Reed of Missouri in a debate in 1913, 'why there should be any sympathy or sentiment about a long-legged, long-beaked, long-necked bird that lives in swamps and eats tadpoles, and fish, and crawfish and things of that kind; why we should worry ourselves into a frenzy because some lady adorns her hat with one of its feathers, which appears to be the only use it has.'

The egrets were only one example of the general bird pillage that was carried on across the world. Though, perhaps, none was worse than that which occurred in the United States. In the 1880s breech-loading shotguns were sold commercially in large numbers; in 1893 the repeating shotgun made its appearance. Now no bird was safe, they were shot for food, shot for the market, shot for plumage or skins, or shot for the sheer pleasure of killing. The gulls, widely popular with the millinery trade, were under threat from the Atlantic coast to the Gulf of Mexico where small armies of hunters would descend on nesting and breeding sites and slaughter indiscriminately. By 1900 the once numerous herring gull was a rarity in the eastern part of Long Island Sound. An order from a Paris fashion house for 40,000 pairs of gull's wings led to the complete annihilation of one colony on Cape Cod. The tern, a great favourite for hats in the United States, was chivied from place to place and was particularly vulnerable at nesting time when their reluctance to leave their nests made them easy prey. When shooting failed, baited fishhooks were tried instead. Owls, especially the barred owl whose feathers bleached well, were highly desirable. Whooper and trumpeter swans, quarry for both meat and feather hunters, were almost driven to extinction, and swan's breast skins became a popular trimming.

Elsewhere the ravages were on a phenomenal scale. A raid by Japanese plumage hunters on the island of Laysan off Hawaii, saw the slaughter of half the island's stock of albatross — 300,000 birds — before a United States' Revenue cutter could stop the massacre. Entire colonies of albatross were eliminated from Marcus Island 3,000 miles to the west, off the coast of Japan. Midway Island was 'covered with great heaps of albatross carcasses,' wrote a horrified observer 'which a crew of poachers had left to rot after the quill feathers had been pulled out of each bird.'

Grebe skins from the American Pacific coast were travelling eastwards by the crate load. Seagull wings might only reach 11 cents the pair in New York, but pelican skins could fetch $1 apiece, so this was the signal for a wholesale attack on the pelican population. The roseate spoonbill had been almost annihilated in the United States. In Australia the lyre-bird was nearing the same fate. Only the hummingbird was given a reprieve, as by some whim of fashion they became unpopular with society milliners.

As American bird lovers saw the massacre of the bird life going on around them they looked sorrowfully back on the time when the great heronries teemed with life and when as night approached the air would be 'filled with birds on their way to their homes in the big rookeries. Often the foliage of a key was hidden by the mass of birds, and the island made to look like a huge snow-drift.' or when 'it looked from a distance as if a big white sheet had been thrown over the mangroves.'

In the first three months of 1885, 750,000 birdskins were sold on the London market alone. A single consignment for one London dealer contained 32,000 hummingbirds, 80,000 aquatic birds of all sorts, and no less than 800,000 pairs of assorted wings. For the most part these originated from the West Indies, Brazil and the Orient. Two years later a single London dealer handled an incredible two million birdskins in twelve months. If the London trade was big, the Paris trade was vastly bigger, and that in New York nearly as large. In New York in 1907, $7 million worth of skins and plumage was sold.

Such an enormous and lucrative trade inevitably developed a powerful and influential voice. And it was raised in its full stridency when the inevitable outcry against this mass bird slaughter was raised.

For many years and long before the beginning of this century, scientists had been voicing concern over the evident decline of species. The fondly held view that unlimited reservoirs of stocks of dwindling species existed 'somewhere' were shown up as myths when the scientific study of birds was taken up in earnest and communications to everywhere that might be 'somewhere' improved. It seemed from all evidence that there was a real danger of the elimination of entire populations unless something was done to check the process. On the other hand, as one man expressed it, 'The Good Book says "man shall have dominion over all creatures". They're ourn to use.'

Britain was a forerunner in the protection of birds. Eleven years after the Protection of Seabirds Act in 1869 a general Bird Protection Act was passed. This stopped the despicable practices of the professional bird catchers who used traps, lime and nets to ensnare larks, buntings, finches and other small birds for the cage. In 1884 the first International Ornithological Congress took place in Vienna. In 1885 the Plumage League was formed which led, in 1889, to the foundation of the Society for the Protection of Birds, later to become the Royal Society—whose original aim was to 'stop the enormous destruction of bird life by milliners and others for purely decorative purposes.'

In the United States, parallel bird protection efforts were in train. 1873 saw the foundation of a new magazine entitled *Forest and Stream* and, in 1886, the first Audubon Society was formed. *Forest and Stream* with its blend of game shooting, sportsmanship and nature loving was to assert immense influence in the education of the shooting and hunting fraternity making them aware of the fragile nature of their wild heritage. In 1905 the National Association of Audubon Societies was created, and with it a very powerful conservation voice.

The final solution, however, had to rest on the ending of the plumage market itself. Its final expiry was a long, acrimonious struggle. But by a combination of education, outrage, humanity, and a growing awareness by people of what Nature meant to civilization, the conservers triumphed. 1913 saw the final prohibition of the import of bird skins and plumage into the United States—except for scientific and educational purposes—and onlookers were delighted by the bizarre sight of female visitors returning from Europe bearing bird products on their hats or gowns only to lose their feathers at the scissors of the Customs officials.

Loss of habitat is the primary threat to the continuation of many species of bird today. Every year an astonishing quantity of land is lost to the resident bird life; wetlands are drained to make way for agricultural or industrial development, forest clearing in many parts of the world—particularly of the valuable rain forests of the Amazonian basin—routs out bird and other wildlife altogether and disturbs vastly more.

Bird persecution in many forms still persists, be it of hawks for falconry, or the hoopoe for its supposed aphrodisiacal power. The live bird trade flourishes and a recent estimate has put the size of this trade at over 5,000,000 birds a year. It is well known that some of the catching is humane, but many are caught by barbarous methods and without distinction, and if not in the ideal plumage are killed on the spot. Further mortality occurs in transit, either from the catching areas or due to travel delays or inadequate freighting. Some of these birds are for zoos, bird parks and scientific collections, others are for private use as cagebirds. Egg collecting, usually of the most threatened and, therefore, the most desirable species, is a thriving market. Migratory birds are particularly vulnerable to shooting and trapping. In Turkey and Malta, which are on the direct migratory routes of many birds of prey—hawks,

(Opposite) Birds in transit—a trade that involves over 5,000,000 birds every year.

65 LEMON MALE CANARIES
(SERINUS CANARIES)
65 ORANGE AND MISCELLANEOUS
CANARIES (SERINUS CANARIES)

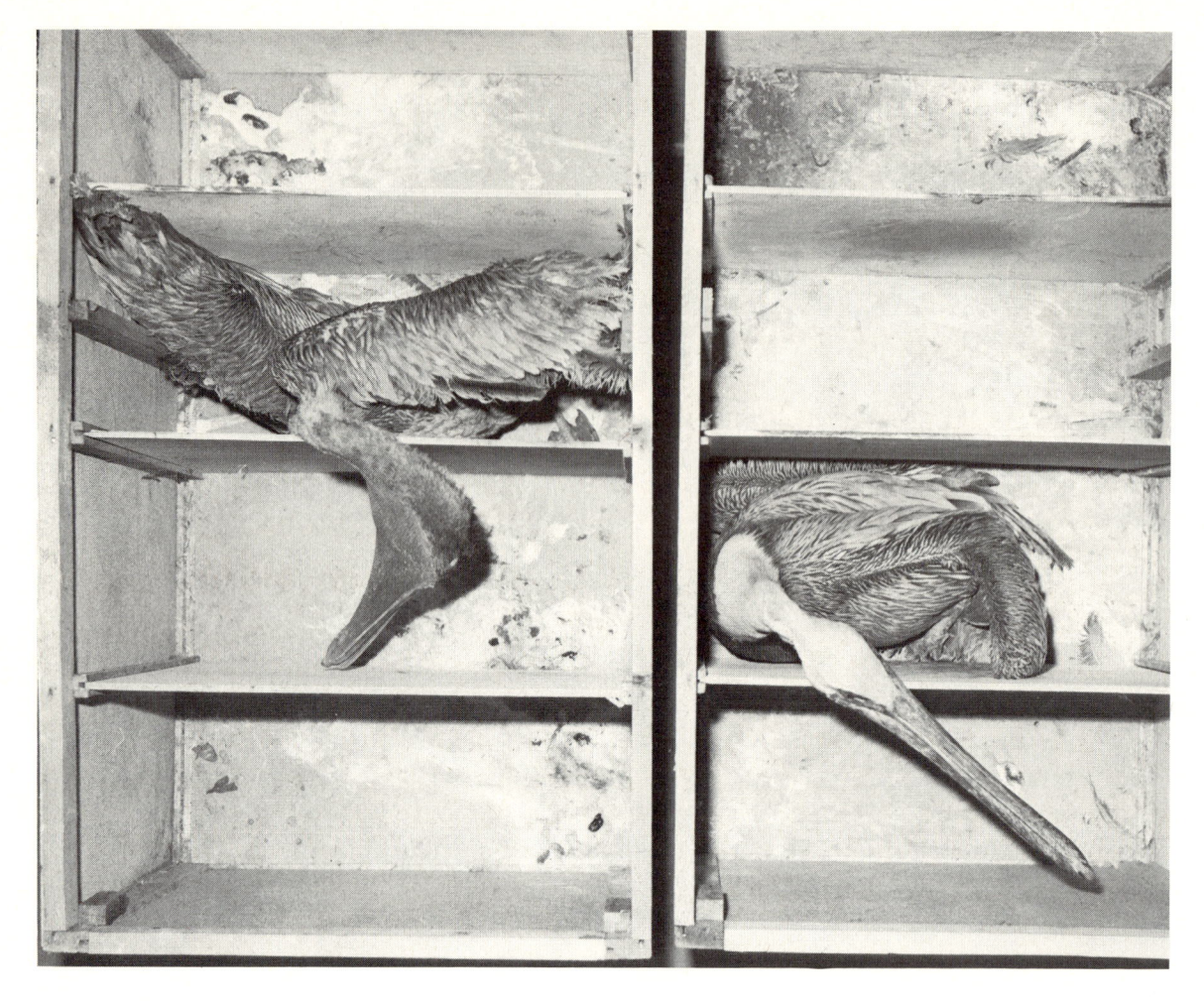

Dead on arrival.

eagles and vultures, it is reckoned that one in three birds of prey that pass over Malta are shot annually. But for sheer size, however, the slaughter of the smaller migratory birds along the shores of the Mediterranean is pre-eminent. As much of this killing is by using indiscriminate methods, rarer species are as much at risk as those of more common varieties.

In France, Spain, Cyprus, Italy, Malta and Turkey the slaughter of migratory songbirds—most killed to satisfy a gourmet's delight for a single tinned or pickled mouthful—is big business. France accounts for between five and ten million head. The small bird hunters of Cyprus capture and kill something between three and seven million. Italy was by far the greatest offender and it is believed that here no less than 240 million birds are killed every year.

'Black Sunday', as the official opening day for migratory bird shooting in Italy has been dubbed, sees a fair proportion of the country's

2,000,000 licenced holders of guns, and nobody knows how many others, set about the songbird slaughter. This shooting, as in the other methods of small bird destruction, is wholly indiscriminate, anything that flies is fair game.

But a recent decision by the Council of Ministers of the European Economic Community could see an end to much of this wanton killing. Under proposals which have now been agreed, all birds are protected except those classified as game birds. Apart from the usual pheasant, partridge, wild duck and those species regularly hunted for sport, has been added skylarks, blackbirds, the mistle and song thrush, redwings and field fares.

At last it would seem that the movement started in Europe in 1869 with the British Seabird Protection Act is beginning to come to fruition.

Netting (in this case a skylark) accounts for many more deaths—a pursuit which recent international agreements look like bringing to an end.

Safari and Shikar: Big Game Hunting

Whereby much Game thereby destroyed to the benefytt of no man.

Edict of King Edward VI of England, 1548

(On this page and opposite) Bear and boar hunting in the Middle Ages (Hans Burgkmaer 1530).

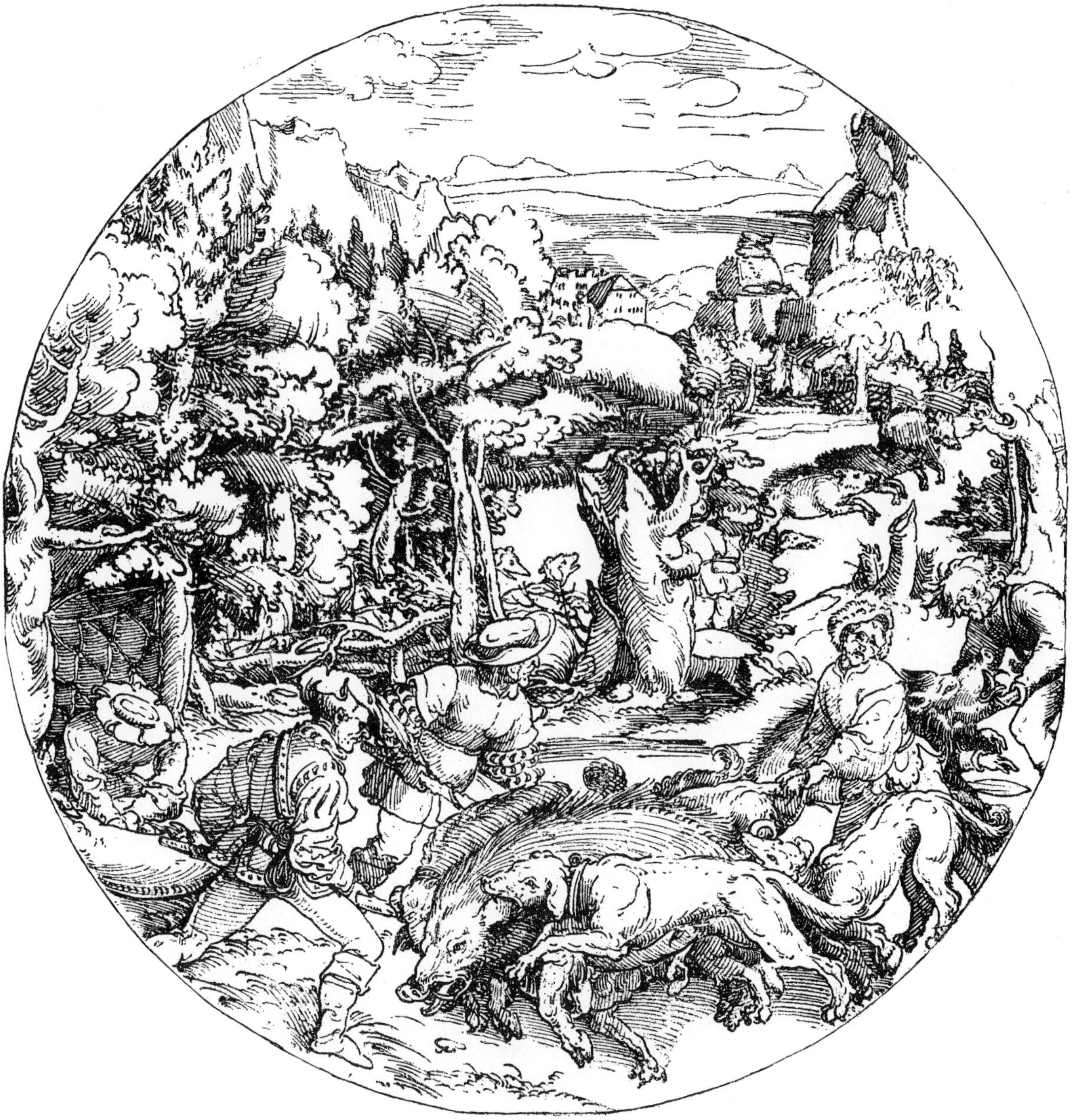

Earliest man had to hunt to exist. Even when he turned to farming, hunting was a necessary part of life, and when hunting was indifferent man often went hungry. Yet even when sheer necessity obviated killing man still hunted. 'There is a passion for hunting, something deeply implanted in the human breast,' wrote Charles Dickens over a century ago. It is something indefinable, as old as time and as deep-rooted as man's nature itself, and it is more than the challenge of the chase, the thrill of handling a weapon, the test of skills, the peace and tranquility of the surroundings, the boon of good cheer and companionship, the return to nature of the city dweller, the primaeval pitting of wits between man and beast. Wrote one Indian big game hunter:

> Often as I toiled over the huge burnt-up wastes, with no tittle of success to reward my efforts, scorched by the burning noonday sun, chilled by the bitter blasts by night, fed on the unappetising productions of a Kashmiri cook, more unsavoury than ever since dung had become the only fuel available, I wondered wherein lay the extraordinary attraction which drew me willy-nilly from the comforts and luxuries of modern life to wander solitary over the dreary tracts of this forbidding land.

Perhaps in pursuit of some record 'head'. And even then, sometimes, the opportunity at last offered might not be taken.

Another hunter wrote:

> I had only to raise my rifle and he was done, when a revulsion of feeling came over me. Why should I kill him? I had won hands down and could exercise my prerogative of mercy, so I stood up and took my hat off to him. For one minute he stood looking at me with his off fore hoof well off the ground, then he was gone and I saw him in the flesh no more. On the wall of my room hang two shields, each carrying the head of one of those two twenty-one inch buck I had shot on that trip. And in the middle, between them hangs an empty shield. On it I often see in imagination the head of the finest black buck I never shot.

The hunting dichotomy is one of the most inexplicable of human emotions. Why cherish and yet kill? Perhaps our primeval consciousness goes back to the days when our ancestors found a natural bond with their quarry, when the casting up of a whale on a beach must have appeared a god-given bounty. Or a successful hunt of mammoth or mastodon was an event of celebration as there would be food and hides in plenty and bones to make the implements by which they lived. Little the wonder that they worshipped the animals they hunted and which could provide so many of their needs.

Early societies in many parts of the world formed close religious–mystical links with their quarry, and such associations saved many species from unnecessary slaughter. The bear cult was the basis for such worship in Japan, Siberia and alpine Europe. The fox was sacred in Peru and with the Chimu, the forerunners of the Aztecs of Central America. The tiger was treated with reverence in Siberia, and offerings were left for him as an act of obeisance. Thus tiger claws were made into amulets to ward off the evil eye, his skin gave the owner power over his adversaries and a tiger's tooth was an infallible passport to continuing virility. Some societies saw certain animals as messengers of the gods, and these must be preserved at all costs. Others looked on them as being the reincarnation of their own ancestors. Primitive tribes still hold such deep mystical relationships with the animals they hunt. Hunting traditions and hunting rituals and ceremony, the formal laying out of game today, the sounding of the 'morte' for the souls of the dead beasts—at one and the same time a salute to their courage and a invocation for good sport in the future—are not far removed from similar rites performed by our ancestors.

To primitive understandings, the happenings of nature and thus the work of their gods could only be interpreted through the behaviour of animals they knew. Sometimes the god was incarnate as an animal. In Hindu mythology Vishnu might be seen as an elephant or boar holding up the world. Earthquakes, the most terrifying of natural events and wholly without rational explanation to primitive minds, were variously attributed to the restless stirrings of a world-carrying tortoise (the Algonquins of North America), a frog (Mongolia), a hog (the Celebes). In Siberia the presence of colossal mammoth deposits, which were exploited as ivory in the earlier years of this century, led the inhabitants to believe that these huge beasts still existed and it was their tramping below the ground that caused the frequent earth shudders that shook their world.

As their gods were associated with animals, so their gods on earth, their kings, rulers, emperors or princes were looked on as possessing the god-like gifts of an animal, and the animal itself granted divine status. Thus in Benin in West Africa it was the leopard who was regarded as their king's special talisman. In Assyria the lion was accounted as royal quarry and Ashburnipal, who reigned in the seventh century BC, delighted in the killing of caged lions in a form of ritual slaughter. In ancient Egypt the pharaohs were great hunters. Ramses III was recorded for all posterity as a mighty hunter, 'With my own hand, I the Pharaoh killed from a chariot 102 wild-eyed lions.'

Hunting was a proof of manhood and of warlike skills, of courage and horsemanship besides. Sir Thomas More wrote:

Manhood I am, therefore I me delyght
To hunt and hawke, to nourish up and fede,
The greyhounds to the course, the hawk to th' flyght
And to Bestryde a good and lusty stede;
These thynges become a very man in dede.

Ioan. Stradanus invent.

Ioan. Collaert scul.   Phls Galle excu.

Early man's weapons were crude. The bow and arrow, spear or javelin, the pit and the net, could hardly, one might think, encompass the extinction or elimination of a species, although fire, used by many societies, was a true instrument of mass destruction. Yet over the centuries and with only these primitive weapons at their disposal, man, in many cultures, wiped out entire populations of wild animals. The ancestors of the North American Indian killed off the forerunners of the buffalo. The Assyrians saw to the virtual disappearance of the lion in their country, as did the Greeks in theirs. As civilization advanced and as agricultural settlements encroached on the wildernesses, so the indigenous wild animals retreated, firstly into the wilder recesses of the country and then, if hunted too assiduously, they were simply wiped out. For many in Europe and elsewhere, particularly in the Mediterranean region, hunting was no longer a necessity, it was a pastime and a sport, a spectacle of unrivalled magnificence.

In the days of the Pharaohs, hunting in Egypt sometimes took on the form of ritual and spectacle, with herds of game driven towards waiting

The hunt — King Sardanapal of Assyria.

nets and ending in an orgy of killing. The Assyrians and Persians possessed game parks where only the most privileged might hunt and within these preserves game sweeps would take place with animal casualties numbered in thousands. But the accolade of such animal slaughter was reserved for the Romans.

The *venationes* preceded the great gladiatorial contests which the Romans loved. Many Romans professed a deep love of nature, yet these killing orgies attained a huge popularity. Beast against beast, or beast against man, sometimes man against man, but killing and spectacle were the twin themes. Animal slaying was to become a feature of the many festivals that peppered the Roman calendar.

The quarry were often native animals, but the 'exotic' were the more popular—lions from Syria or Libya, Mesopotamia or Arabia, bears from Asia Minor, Greece or Armenia (those from Persia were renowned for their ferocity; Spanish or occasionally Scottish bears were added to give extra flavour to the dish provided for the blood-hungry spectators). Ostriches came from Libya (with singular inappropriateness they

Capture by deception.

were once referred to as *passer marinus*: the sparrow from overseas), leopards were sent from Cilicia. The most distant reaches of the Empire were combed to satisfy the gory appetites of the Roman populace.

The slaughter was often on the grand scale. The first recorded *venationes* was in 186 BC, and they flourished for over 800 years until the empire perished. In 55 BC, Pompey showed and saw slaughtered 20 elephants, 600 lions, 410 female leopards, as well as huge numbers of lynx and monkeys. In 25 BC, Servilius produced a theatrical spectacle which involved the slaying of 300 bears and a similar number of wild animals, most of them from Africa. Successive Roman rulers strove to outdo their predecessors in the gory originality of the spectacles they lay before the Roman populace, for this was an outward symbol of their own power as the chosen of men, and man's power over the kingdom of the beasts. Thus Caligula was once responsible for the killing of 400 bears and 400 other wild animals. Nero was an avid enthusiast and on one occasion invited the senators to come and help with the killing in the arena.

In the year AD 80, to celebrate the opening of the huge Colosseum, Titus masterminded a festival which lasted for 100 days. On the first

The Roman Circus was to witness some of the most gory animal spectacles in history. Illustration from Le Dictionnaire du Théâtre *by Arthur Pugin.*

Man pitted against Beast.

day 5,000 animals were exhibited, and many slain, and over the ensuing weeks a further 9,000 were despatched. Killing in the arena was usually reserved for the professional animal slayers, but this time as an added attraction, women were allowed to join in. Even this monumental slaughter, though, was outdone by Trajan who in honour of his Dacian triumph presided over the slaughter of no less than 11,000 animals in 120 days of continuous massacre.

To satisfy this hunger for animal victims, hunting parties were sent to the furthest corners of the Empire. These teams were professional hunters. The animals had to be taken alive, transported across the water and arrive in good condition in Italy. They were put in transit houses, *vivaria*, and kept there half-starved to make them fierce until the time came for them to appear at the Colosseum or wherever they were needed. Then they were brought to cages beneath or behind the arena the night preceding the *venationes*.

This continual traffic in captured animals started to have the inevitable effect on animal stocks in many parts of the Empire, and particularly in the Mediterranean area. The elephant was all but wiped out in Libya and Tunisia. The crocodile was no longer to be found on the lower reaches of the Nile. By the birth of Christ, and the reign of Augustus, the lion in Libya was an uncommon animal. By the second century AD both lion and leopard were almost hunted out of much of North Africa and the Middle East, and elsewhere were generally so scarce that greater quantities of deer and other common species were used to make up numbers in the killing.

The gladatorial combat came to a halt around the fourth century AD, but the *venationes* persisted until the final collapse of the Roman Empire in AD 681.

Sport for all.

Never again were such spectacles to be witnessed, although slaughter on a huge scale was to take place in many lands, and occasionally with as much theatre. In Europe by the eighth century, the hunt had reached a high degree of sophistication and reserves were established for the exclusive few. Within these reserves the killing of deer and other forest denizens was the prerogative of king, lord or noble and the penalty for transgression ruthless. For the most part hunting was a personal sport, with hound and horse, and a few followers. Occasionally a drive or *battue* was organized and deer would be gathered and herded towards the waiting hunters.

Such killing was generally on a small scale and restricted to royal game parks where the quarry was probably numerous, and there was little danger of the elimination of an entire species in an area. The weapons were still the bow and arrow, spear and knife. Hand to claw combat with bear or wolf, or in parts of North Africa and the Middle East, with lion or leopard were not unknown. The cross-bow was also used in sport, and it was so light that a lady could wield it. But this innovation was nothing to the appearance of the 'handgonne', which in its many developing guises was to revolutionize hunting as it was war.

'Handgonnes' had made their appearance as early as the sixteenth century and in their crudeness were likely to be as lethal to the user as to any enemy or quarry. From time to time royal edicts were issued prohibiting their use. But the gun as a sporting weapon was here to stay, and with it an entirely new phase of the war was opened in the conflict between man and animal.

These early guns were cumbersome weapons. Muzzle-loading with long barrels which needed to be supported by a forked stick, they were fired with a slow fuse—which occasioned an interval between firing and discharge—and later with match or flintlock. Rarely would the quarry obligingly wait while the hunter sighted, fired and the bullet actually left the barrel. It was better by far to have the game driven towards the hunter. Thus evolved the grisly spectacles which characterized mass hunting in the seventeenth and early eighteenth centuries.

In order to slow down the game, many were driven into nets where they could be destroyed at leisure; sometimes other devices were employed. The approaching game might be channelled so as to arrive en masse for the waiting hunters, or, occasionally more elaborate massacres were provided and the deer and other forest creatures collected in from miles around and driven forward by hordes of beaters and foresters. Perhaps directed towards a false painted landscape and as they reached it they fell into a lake, river or artificial pond and while swimming to the further side would make an easy mark for the waiting guns and provide a delicious spectacle to the on-lookers sitting in specially created galleries overlooking the killing ground. This debased form of hunting spectacle was known as the 'water jump' and in subtle diversifications became a popular form of 'disport'.

But even with these activities, game was still amazingly plentiful in much of Europe. It is true that despite several attempts to reintroduce the creature into the royal forests, the boar was no longer to be found in England. The lynx, long persecuted, had retreated into the more remote fastnesses in western Europe, as had the bear. But the main quarry, deer buck, fox, roe, hare, and in Europe the boar, were still to be found in almost untouched profusion. The royal preserve, with its stringent penalties for poaching, undoubtedly saved many species from at least local extinction.

In olden times these reserves covered vast tracts of country in many lands. In ancient China deer parks were set aside for the sport of the mighty (they also had 'parks of intelligence', a forerunner of the menagerie and zoo of today). Europe saw the creation of forest preserves as long ago as the days of Charlemagne. By the eighteenth century closed seasons were in force in a number of countries, particularly in Spain where their views on game preservation for hunting were highly advanced. Poachers were swiftly dealt with. The humane punishment of a heavy fine for poaching in the days of Charlemagne, by 1500 had been succeeded by rigid, and cruelly efficient retribution under Maximilian I.

This form of conservation—although the conservation purist would condemn it as being survival for the wrong reasons—acted as a regulator. It was the forerunner to the increasing modern trend in game farming. With the elimination of predators in the interest of the expanding farming communities, such preserving, culling and control was essential to healthy continuance of game stocks.

The hunter today has an increasing responsibility as a regulator, for Darwin's natural selection has been superseded by man's selection. The process is now one of thinning rather than purely the removal of the weak and sickly. It is essential to prevent overcrowding, to have only enough stock for the amount of available food. And the hunter must now be looked on as an essential ingredient in maintaining the artificial balance man has created with nature and his natural surroundings.

As effective as royal edicts and royal preserves, were those regulations forbidding the taking of specific animals except by privileged classes. Not only with the quarry, also with the means of taking it. Social etiquette was strict:

An Eagle for an Emperor
A Gerfalcon for a King
A Peregrine for an Earl
A Merlyon [Merlin] for a Lady
A Goshawk for a Yeoman
A Sparehawk [Sparrowhawk] for a Priest
A Musket [Male Sparrowhawk] for a Priest's clerk
A Kestrel for a Knave.

To the early North American colonists, the amount of wild game that abounded in the woods around their settlements seemed limitless. It was one of the bounties of God that he had 'Furnished this country with all sorts of wild beasts and fowls, which every one hath an interest in and may hunt at his pleasure, where, besides the pleasure of hunting, he may furnish his house with excellent fat venison, turkies, heath-hens, cranes, swans, ducks and the like,' wrote an early settler, amazed and delighted at the profusion of game on which he could exercise his pleasure.

Faced with such plenty the early colonists went about killing indiscriminately, so indiscriminately that the infant colony of Rhode

144

Island was forced as early as 1646 to introduce a close season for deer. The heath-hen, so abundant at the beginning of the eighteenth century that it was forbidden to feed the servants on the bird more than once or twice a week, by 1840 had disappeared altogether from Long Island, and 50 years later was not to be found anywhere in the states of New York, Virginia or Pennsylvania.

By the beginning of the nineteenth century, Daniel Boone complained that the woods on the eastern side of the country had been largely shot out, and Audubon could write not long afterwards that:

> The different modes of destroying deer are probably too well understood and too successfully practiced in the United States; for notwithstanding the almost incredible abundance of these beautiful animals in our forests and prairies, such havoc is carried on amongst them, that in a few centuries they will probably be as scarce as in America as the great bustard now is in Britain.

Bighorn sheep and mule deer in North Dakota, USA c. 1890.

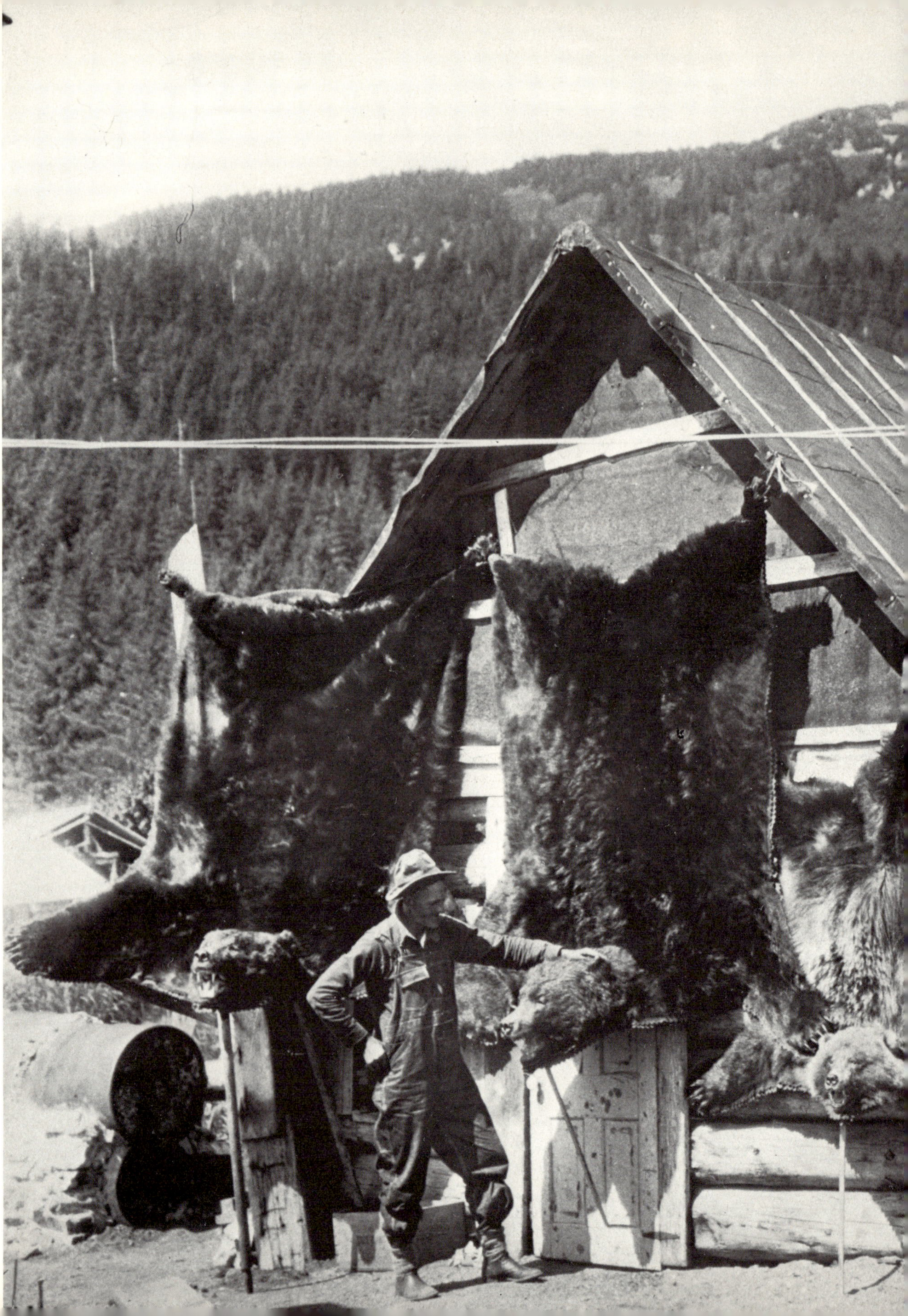

The bear hunter.

Communications then were primitive. Huge tracts of the great continent remained untrodden by the white man and enormous stocks of indigenous game remained unmolested. This was all to change with the advent of the railroad. As the great iron way crept ever westward more and more land with unbelievable game riches were opened to the hunter. And the spread of communications coincided with improvements in firearms. The appearance of the breech-loading shotgun and the repeating rifle rang the death knell for thousands of head of game in many countries, and to bring some species to the brink of extinction.

And in America, spurred on by the example of Theodore Roosevelt, hunting became a passion. Roosevelt wrote:

> The chase is the best of all national pastimes, and this is none the less because like every other pastime it is a mere source of weakness if carried on in an unhealthy manner, or to an excessive degree, or under artificial conditions ... The conditions of modern life are highly artificial and too often tend to a softening of fibre, physical and moral. It is a good thing to be forced to show self-reliance, resourcefulness in emergency, willingness to endure fatigue and hunger, and at need to face risk. Hunting is praiseworthy very much as it develops these qualities.

Hunting under the right 'conditions' was desperately needed in America, for game was being wiped out to an alarming degree. Already by the 1850s the moose was a rarity in the eastern states. There were a few still surviving in northern Maine, but in the Adirondacks where formerly they had been plentiful, they were nothing but a memory.

In order to develop Roosevelt's tenets of sportsmanship and the benefits of an outdoor life, the Boone and Crockett Club—named after America's most famous sons of the forest—was created in 1887 'to promote manly sport with the rifle', and more generally to develop and perpetuate reliability, energy, resolution, self-confidence and self-reliance.

Duck hunting 1916.

These sentiments were echoed to the full by the early big-game hunters in Africa, a land which was at first a game paradise. When Jan van Riebeck landed at the Cape of Good Hope in 1652 it was to find hippo, black rhino, elephant, lion and leopard as well as many kinds of antelope in vast quantities. There were eland on Table Mountain, and the remarkable quagga in immense herds on the plains. Nearly 200 years later, in 1837 when Queen Victoria came to the throne of England, much of the northern part of what was then Cape Colony was still an uninhabited wilderness occupied only by vast herds of game. Blesbok, hartebeest, wildebeest, gemsbok, springbok and the ubiquitous quagga roamed the Karoos in their hundreds of thousands. Towards the Orange River the lion could be found in great quantity. On the eastern fringe of the territory the ivory hunters were killing elephant almost within sight of the sea.

Beyond the Orange River lay a largely unknown land which had been penetrated by few white men, except a number of hardy missionaries and a few early game hunters, who combined their sport with discovery and exploration. Otherwise the country and the animals had been largely untouched.

Giraffe hunting from William Cornwallis Harris's Wild Sports of Southern Africa.

Among this intrepid band of pioneers was William Cornwallis Harris who in 1836 struck inland for six months on a hunting expedition bearing with him 18,000 lead bullets, pig lead to make more and a full barrel of gunpowder. And what he saw and discovered was a fairyland of game. He wrote:

149

We passed over a low tract about eight miles in extent, strongly impregnated with salt, and abounding in lakes and pools. The number of wild animals almost realised fable, the roads made by their incessant tramp resembling so many well-travelled highways. At every step incredible herds of blesbucks, and springbucks, with troops of gnus and squadrons of the common or stripeless quagga, were performing their complicated evolutions; and not infrequently a knot of ostriches, decked in their white plumes, played the part of general officer and staff with such propriety as still further to remind the spectator of a cavalry review.

Of these animals the quagga sounds a creature of fiction. A relative of the zebra, it was called *wilde esel* or wild ass by the Boer, to distinguish it from the *wilde paard* or wild horse, the zebra. Its name derived from the Hottentot *quacha*, in turn a literal translation of its high-pitched cry. It was often confused by early hunters with the *bontequagga* or Burchell's zebra, a creature also made extinct in the nineteenth century.

The quagga was an animal that could be easily domesticated and from time to time was driven in harness. Indeed in the 1810s in London, a Sheriff Parsons drove a pair of quagga in his carriage. In its native habitat it frequented the open plains in large herds. It was also good to eat and its hide was immensely tough and hard wearing. And these were the twin causes for its demise. Such an easily available and accessible creature was heaven-sent to the Boers for feeding native labour. And those that were not shot for food were slaughtered by the hide hunters. The last quagga in South Africa was believed shot in 1858 and the sole survivor, in Amsterdam Zoo, died in 1883.

Trophies c. 1880.

In 1836 commenced the Great Trek which was to take the Boer inland to Natal, the Transvaal and the Orange Free State. And with it started the systematic elimination of game in South Africa.

By 1840 the eland was all but shot out of the southern reaches of the country. 1842 saw the lion, once so numerous that 200 had been shot on the Trek, shot out south of the Orange River. The bontebok, which inhabited the plains by the sea, was almost eliminated. The blesbok, source of huge numbers of skins for the London hide market, was practically wiped out. The Boer farmers and hide hunters were the principal wielders of destruction. 'Scarcely an hour elapsed at morning, noon or eve, but the distant booming of the Dutchman's gun saluted the ear,' wrote an English settler, as the Boer's long-barreled *roers* continued the game slaughter.

Ivory, hides and ostrich plumes were the principal exports in the first half of the nineteenth century, but the source of this bounty was becoming scarce. By the 1850s nowhere within the country was any appreciable quantity of elephant and other game to be found less than several hundred miles from the coast, and usually a great deal further inland than that. The once vast herds had been broken up, dispersed, decimated and scattered across the country by incessant shooting and constant disturbance.

By 1870 there were no elephant, except a few forlorn survivors south of the Zambezi River; most had sought sanctuary in the tse-tse zone to the north where it was death to bring a horse and where there was, if only temporarily, peace.

These were what the African big-game hunters looked on as the great days of game hunting. It was the era of such men as Oswell, Vardon, Baldwin and Selous, the last of the great African hunters. Many of the early explorers and naturalists combined hunting with their more scientific studies, men such as the Swedes, Sparrman and Thunberg, or the remarkable Frenchman, Le Vaillant, who went on his travels accompanied by a monkey for companionship and a tame cock to wake him in the mornings and invariably carried with him an astonishing armoury consisting of a pair of double-barrelled pistols in the side pockets of his breeches, another pair at his belt, his 'double-barrelled fusee' slung at the bow of his saddle, an enormous sabre at his side and a dagger hanging from his neck on a cord. Of it he said himself, 'This arsenal incommoded me considerably at first; but I never quitted it, both on account of my own safety, and because by this precaution I seemed to increase the confidence of my people.' On his journey back to the Cape he came across what must have been one of the most amazing natural phenomena in the country, the annual migration of the springbok, the *trek-bokken* of the Boers. Le Vaillant reckoned he saw a modestly estimated 50,000 springbok on the move migrating from the dry rocky regions in the south for some woody watered region in the north.

Another spectator on another occasion described this astonishing sight:

> This was I think, the most extraordinary and striking scene, as connected with beasts of the chase, I ever beheld. For about two hours before dawn I had been lying awake in my waggon, listening to the grunting of the bucks within two hundred yards of me, imagining that some large herd of springboks was feeding beside my camp; but rising when it was light, and looking about me, I beheld the ground to the northward of my camp actually covered with a dense living mass of springboks, marching slowly and steadily along; they extended from an opening in the long range of hills on the west, through which they continued pouring, like the flood of some great river, to a ridge about a mile to the north-east, over which they disappeared—the breadth of ground they covered might have been somewhere about half a mile. I stood upon the fore-chest of my waggon for nearly two hours, lost in astonishment.

The *trek-bokken* would virtually lay waste the land over which it passed.

The writings of the early hunters show that in their way many 'loved' nature, they sought it and respected it, and often they were very close to it indeed. At one moment they could glory in the sight of herd after herd of wild game, not for the hunting it promised but for the magnificence of the spectacle, and at the next the sight of a well-tusked elephant would equally arouse their hunting instinct. People laughed cynically when the Fauna Preservation Society (founded as the Society for the Preservation of the Wild Fauna of the Empire) was created in the early 1900s, and dubbed it the Society of Repentant Butchers as so many one-time big game hunters featured on its founding panel.

Although the depredations of such men were considerable, rarely were they enough to threaten the survival of a species nor to completely strip an area of its game. But taken in conjunction with killing to make way for agriculture, and the other threats to the game of Africa from 1870 onwards, the activities of white hunters were a luxury the game stocks could not afford.

But except for the professional men these big-game hunters were seldom on the scene for more than a few months. It was the settlers who eliminated game for eating, for hides and in the interests of their own farming. But their inroads were more than matched by those of the other indigenous slayer—the native hunter—spurred on by the unquenchable demand for ivory, horns and hides and who was now equipped with guns to achieve it. For the explorers and missionaries had been followed by the traders, and it was they who largely saw to the astonishing decrease of game in much of Africa.

Still the country was relatively unknown. Communications were primitive or non-existent. The opening of the railways made vulnerable huge areas of hitherto untapped game country and with it started the influx of the big-game hunter, the creation of the safari and the birth of the white hunter. A breed which came to notice in 1909 during the well-publicized trip of ex-President Theodore Roosevelt to Kenya, which as a scientific expedition encompassed the destruction of an astonishing bag of game animals.

The 1920s and 1930s were to see the worst period of game killing in Africa, especially East Africa. This was the era of the pseudo-sportsman who might shoot game while smoking a pipe and reclining in a hammock borne by native servants, and who slaughtered purely for the pleasure of killing, rarely even collecting the meat of the slain animals. With the coming of the motor-car the word 'safari' also took on a new meaning. As one disgruntled hunter scathingly put it, 'All this makes a farce of the whole thing and it only means the so-called "big-game hunter" comes back at the end of six weeks with a fine bag obtained with practically no work, absolutely no hardship and very little danger.' The 'champagne safari' was all the rage. It looked as though an earlier prophecy that game in Africa was likely not to be shot out, but murdered out was nearing reality.

Lion hunting in Africa in the 1890s.

153

Another profound effect on game numbers in the 1930s up to the 1950s was the slaughter designed to eliminate the tse-tse fly. Game animals were potential carriers and hundreds of thousands were eliminated in Uganda, Rhodesia, South Africa, Tangyanika and Kenya. Today, despite attempts at game regulation and the potential profit from a thriving tourist and hunting traffic, poaching of a mounting sophistication and intensity is causing grave concern to game conservationists in many parts of Africa.

Hunting the tiger.

Game regulations came late to Africa, but in the other major home of big-game hunting, India, game shooting had long been under strict and beneficial control.

From the earliest days of the British East India Company, the profusion of game of all sorts amazed and delighted the European. Here were tiger, pig, deer of many different sorts, and birds—peacocks, quail, snipe, duck and many other varieties in incredible, unbelievable profusion. India was a true sportsman's paradise with some of the finest game ground in the world. So in a land where the natives were on the whole both friendly and enthusiastic participants and where time seemed of no account, it is hardly surprising that the then upholders of the Raj, the British sway in India, turned to sport as their principal, indeed together with the game of polo and the sport of pig-sticking, almost their only form of relaxation and amusement.

In the early days there were no limits, no regulations, no restrictions. The whole of the vast sub-continent lay open to the pleasure of the hunters on *shikar*. In fact it was part of the general policy of land clearance for agricultural use which was being pursued in many parts of the country that the game should be eliminated and driven out before work could begin. The white man joyfully joined in the programme.

Early hunting was conducted with spear or knife. The *shikar* was a testing ground of manhood, a proving ground for the nerve and steel of an officer, for this was a pursuit almost exclusively reserved for the officer and administrative classes. If he could stand his ground when attacked by a wrathsome bear, he was unlikely to show cowardice when the Afridi or Pathan attacked his small force. The understatement inherent in the following account sums up well the excitement and danger of the *shikar*.

One officer, a Lieutenant Etherton, who set forth in 1909 on a remarkable hunting foray which took him over 4,000 miles from India over the Himalayas, the Pamirs and across what was then Chinese Turkistan to the trans-Siberia railway, and so back to England, was confronted by two large and very ferocious bears. One he wounded, the other he missed, but both were roused to fury.

> At the second shot both pulled themselves together and with much ominous growling charged straight towards us. The Kalmuk (his guide) with a piercing yell took safety in precipitate flight, leaving me to face the music, which I made some attempt to do. Unfortunately, I had that day only brought five cartridges, hardly sufficient for the job in hand. It is difficult to describe one's feeling at such a moment as this. The sight of two large and ferocious bears sweeping down intent on tearing one to pieces, and the critical situation thus engendered cannot be depicted in mere words. There was no time to lose. I mentally resolved to do the best and account for, at any rate, one of the gigantic creatures with the three rounds now left to me, in the lingering hope of being able to settle for the other with the butt end of my rifle, truly a desperate chance. Both shots at the charging bruins were missed.

By some piece of fortune the firing had the desired effect and the two angry bears turned and ran into the woods, leaving a mightily relieved sportsman . . . Etherton continued, 'I returned to camp sad and silent, not unmixed with disgust, at the brilliant opportunity I had missed of securing a unique bag.'

The early unrestricted shooting could not last. The seemingly

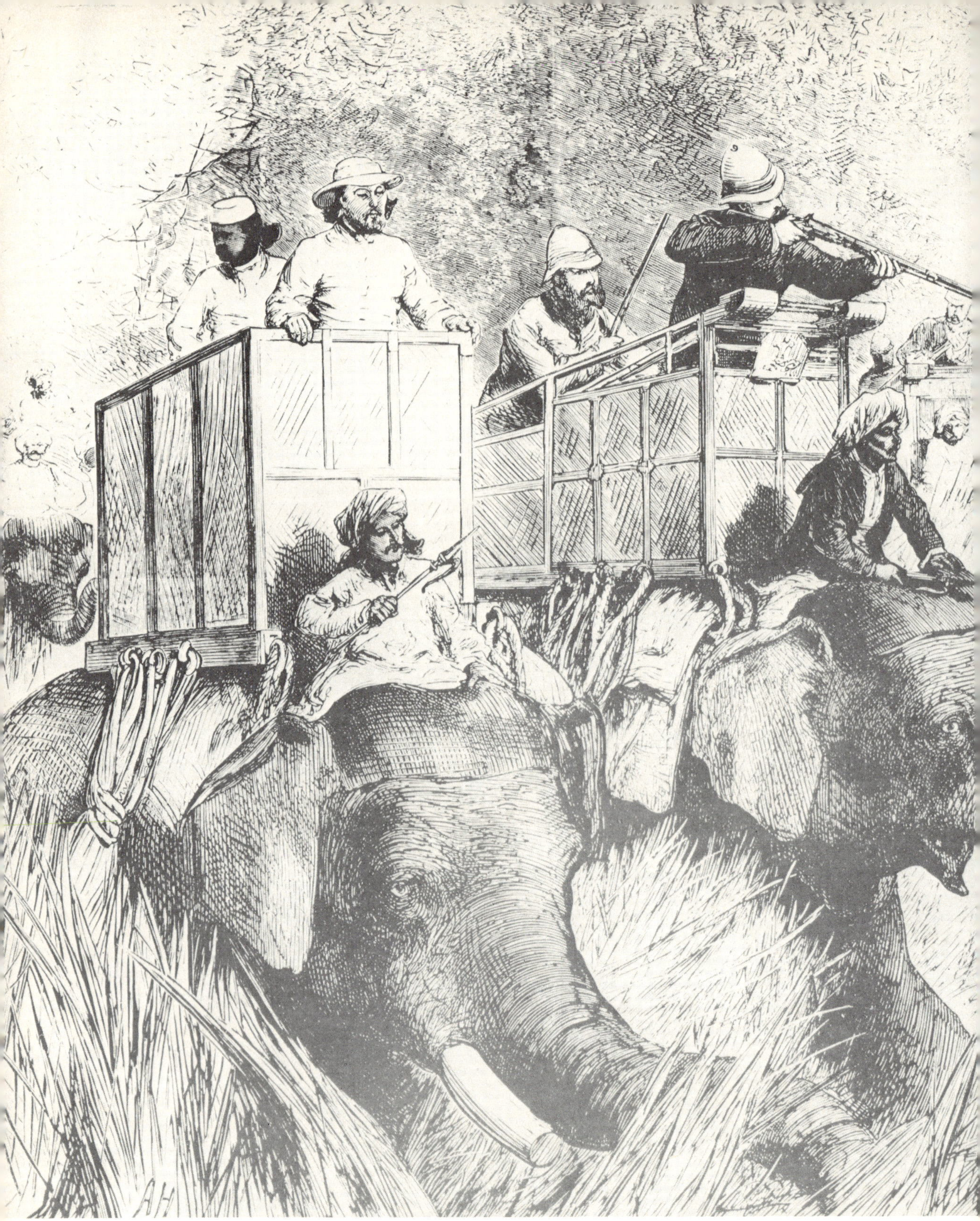

Tiger drive.

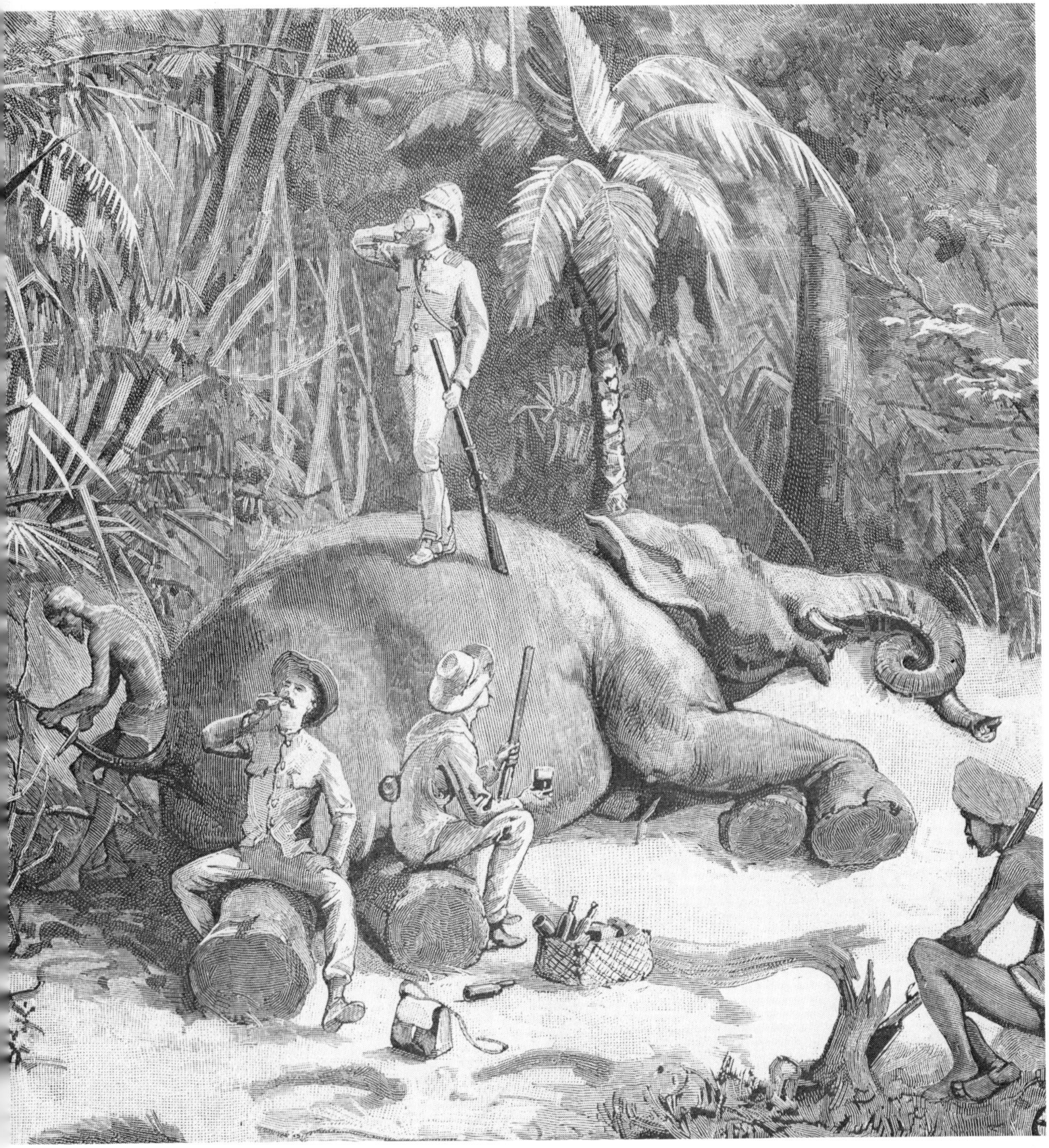

limitless quantities of Indian game began to decrease under the pressures of the *shikar* and of the unfettered hunting of the great Indian princes. The principal quarry was tiger and the many sorts of deer, but other game was also hunted. By 1840 the Indian rhino was becoming rare and within 50 years restricted to a narrow belt in northern India and Nepal. The elephant was rarely shot, except in Ceylon, for easily tamed and domesticated it was too valuable for sport and the thick jungle which it frequented was usually too remote for the average sportsman.

In 1880 game laws were passed and the keepering of the forests placed in the capable hands of the India Forest Service. Then ensued a period of the generally orderly pursuit of what would now be called game cropping. Every officer was entitled to two month's leave and many would spend almost all this time on *shikar*. After much pondering they would decide what game they would like to pursue and having applied for permission be granted a block of forest. Within that area the forest officer would lay down what the hunter could or could not shoot, and within those bounds the hunter was free to operate. Sport in those days required skill, a deep knowledge of nature and the quarry they pursued, endurance and courage, for everywhere there was an element of danger. Above all else, though, it required sportsmanship. Sportsmen were expected to know their wildlife, the novice was encouraged to understand nature—on many occasions his own life and those of his bearers depended on it. It was an attitude as rigid in its compliance as the hunting rules prevalent in parts of Europe today. For he was bound by rules of conduct whose transgression brought instant ostracism from the society in which he moved. There was a heavy fine for shooting the wrong animal, but this was nothing to the contempt of his brother officers or companions.

Many of these hunters developed a keen eye for the beauty of nature, and many of them wrote movingly of their experiences. One man came suddenly on a leopard, 'made of velvet, rubber and steel springs, supple as a snake and nearly as wicked looking.' There it was 'poised for its fatal spring, every muscle rippled beneath the beautiful silver body. The eyes flashed emerald, and the whole figure seemed as though poured from some gigantic ladle of molten silver.' Many also found themselves caught in the coils of the hunting dichotomy. Another wrote, 'your heart swells with joy and pride at securing a good specimen of the finest trophy in India, feelings soon to be replaced by an uncomfortable one of shame and sorrow at destroying so splendid and gallant life.'

For the most part those on *shikar* were not ruthless unbridled slaughterers. They would kill surely, but this killing was tempered by the laws written and unwritten within which they operated, a code of conduct dictated primarily by conscience. Sportsmanship was defined by the great shooting writer Sir Ralph Payne-Gallway in his classic *Instructions to Young Sportsmen* written in 1890, as 'A man who is

(Opposite) In Ceylon the elephant was regarded as a pest.

endowed with a true feeling of sport will always endeavour to give his game a chance—I can think of no better word to express what I mean . . .' This is the essence of hunting to many the world over and these early Nimrods would be speechless with contempt and revulsion at the trend now prevalent in the United States for game ranches.

Many of the early sportsmen found their sport the hard way. Theodore Roosevelt's friend and hunting companion of many years standing, General Hampton, killed over 50 bears in his life, for the most part with no other weapon than a knife. Sir Samuel Baker, administrator, explorer and sportsman, hunted elephant in Ceylon where they were a major pest in the rice fields with a weapon of enormous power, but tackled boar and leopards armed only with a cut-down claymore. On one occasion when charged by a buffalo he found that he had used up his last ball, so coolly loading his gun with 'three shillings' worth of small change' which he had in his pocket, he shot at the charging beast and so stunned it that he was able to make his escape.

Of all the animals that made the sportsman's blood race, the Bengal tiger was pre-eminent. Sport to many in India *was* the tiger, and 100 years ago tiger abounded. It was also a menace. In the 1860s in Bengal alone the tiger was thought to have killed upwards of 2,000 humans each year. Tigers were a common sight on the roads and often a threat to a community (the fat of the dead animals was prized by villagers for treating rheumatism). On the other hand tigers kept down the numbers of the principal crop raiders, deer, pig and monkeys. Thus it was an important matter when hunting came under regulation to limit the number of tigers that might be shot, and even more important to regulate the number of firearms issued to farmers for crop protection. For in inexpert hands the likelihood was to wound rather than kill a tiger, and then it might turn man-eater.

Some of the early hunters speared tigers, but the practice soon disappeared in favour of shooting from a 'machan' or platform in a tree over a bait, or from the swaying howdah mounted on an elephant in a tiger drive. Tiger shooting involved pitting wits against one of the wiliest beasts of the jungle, with the added spice that the hunter might be deflected from his sport to deal with a man-eater which was menacing a village community. This was a challenge invariably accepted, and it added a certain edge to the hunt to know that this time the quarry had already tasted human meat and sought more.

Some estimates put the tiger population in India on the eve of Independence in 1947 as high as 40,000 or even 70,000. Even if this figure is suspect, certainly a very large number of tigers did exist then. This, despite the game shooting of generation after generation of British officers and officials, and the far greater depredations of the maharajahs, some of whom could boast a personal tally of more than 1,000 tigers to their own guns.

Independence was the signal for what was described as a general 'war against animals'. The aftermath of the Japanese war had left behind a small arsenal of weapons. The birth throes of two newly emerging nations placed these and other weapons in the hands of anyone who could handle them, and very many who could not handle them correctly. And game was slaughtered wholesale. If the massacre was not quite on the scale of that of the buffalo in North America it was almost as proportionately destructive.

Already a victim of habitat loss, the unfortunate tiger deprived of much of its legitimate food by the general destruction of game, turned to attacking domestic cattle, and at once became the target of everyman's wrath. In addition it was poisoned and trapped. Most destructive of all was the hunting down by night using a cross-country vehicle, a spotlight and a high-powered rifle.

To add to the general reduction of tiger stocks, hunting tours were highly popular for rich sportsmen in the 1950s, and with tiger skins fetching $1,000 on the market, the inducement was overwhelming.

A nine-foot skin. Between 1947 and the present day the wild tiger population has declined from an estimated 40–70,000 to less than 2,000.

161

Trapping accounted for many deaths.

In 1970 the Indian authorities placed a ban on the export of tiger skins and, in concert, a number of countries banned their importation. A partial remedy and one widely ignored at first, it came only just in time. For the many thousands of tigers on the Indian sub-continent had been, by 1969, reduced to under 3,000 specimens. Thus in 1970 the tiger became a threatened species.

In 1973 'Project Tiger' was mounted by the Indian Government in concert with conservation agencies across the world, principally the World Wildlife Fund. By then the population of Bengal tigers in the wild was under 2,000. Nine reserves (which were later expanded to 11) were established, and within these areas the Indian tiger is beginning to make a come-back.

The situation regarding the other seven species of tiger in existence is more variable. The largest of them all, the Siberian tiger, which can measure ten feet from nose to tail and weigh more than 560 pounds, has a population of probably under 200, and this despite the most stringent conservation moves by the Soviet authorities to preserve an animal which was rare in the 1930s. A further small population also exists in North-East China, but it is believed that this is dwindling. The Chinese tiger proper, which once had a wide range, is probably already facing extinction. The Indo-Chinese tiger, much of whose habitat has been fought over for the past ten years probably now only exists in Malaysia. The Caspian tiger survives as a remnant of under two dozen, and these may well have already disappeared. The Sumatran tiger can be numbered in only a very few hundreds. The Javan tiger numbers less than one dozen specimens. The Bali tiger is already extinct. And that is all of the animal whose range once extended from eastern Turkey to the China Sea, from Siberia to the East Indies, which was once worshipped as a god and earned the tribute: 'to the Lord Tiger who dwelleth in the Forest and the Mountains . . . his Spirit brings happiness to men.'

A Report from the Front

There is no survivor, there is no future, there is no life to be recreated in this form again. We are looking upon the uttermost finality which can be written, glimpsing the darkness which will not know another ray of light. We are in touch with the reality of extinction.

   Arthur Beetle Hough

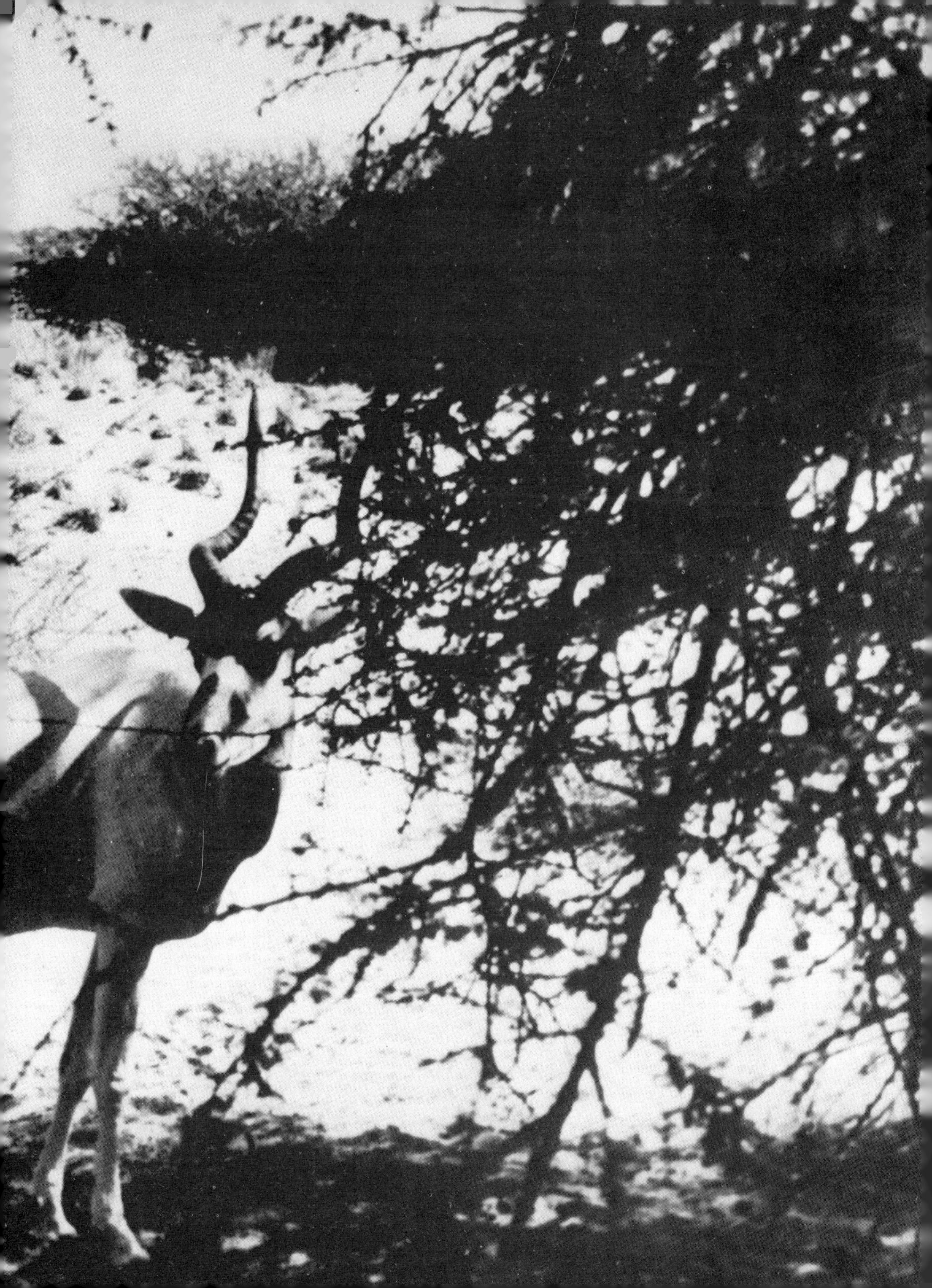

(Previous pages) The addax, once quite common in the deserts of north Africa but hunted down over recent years, is increasingly rare except in the western Sahara. How long will it survive even there?

Although the previous chapters have described some of the major engagements in man's historic war against the animal kingdom, it is a chilling thought that the war still continues, if perhaps in a lower key.

It would seem evident that some species are doomed irrespective of what we do and will pass on anyway, caught in the web of evolution, but in many instances man has speeded the process—it has been estimated that man has quadrupled the extinction rate. For it is no longer a question of restoring the balance of nature, that has gone for good in many parts of the globe; rather, we must try to find an artificial balance and harmony between wild animals and man. This is a process of experiment, and experiment in many areas. Some efforts may be ill-directed, more will be too late, but if the continual probing and researching does not persist our relentless exploitation of nature as the population of man expands, will find us with nothing left.

The weapons man now uses against animals are greater and more diverse than ever they were. Forest clearance, marsh drainage, poor land management and the improvident use of natural resources are problems enough, but add to these the age-old and continuing over-exploitation of animal resources for food, finery or other commercial reasons, the poisoning of land and water by oil, chemical or effluent, and the whole adds up to a catalogue of potential catastrophe. Taking these threats singly it is probable that many animal species would triumph, but with the cumulative threat imposed from so many quarters, in a good number of cases the outcome must be more seriously in doubt.

The existence of what appears to be a comfortable population can often lead to complacency. If that population is confined to a comparatively small area, such as an island or mountain range, it is particularly susceptible to natural calamity or imported disease. Should such a catastrophe strike and population numbers be lowered below the crucial level which seems to be present in some species, oblivion may well be inevitable. The process involved is imprecisely known. It has been suggested that it is almost as though the species concerned is smitten by a death wish, others attribute it to the physical difficulties of male meeting female, but whatever the cause even with captive breeding, if that is successful, survival becomes precarious. A number of passenger pigeons were taken into captivity before the total disappearance of the wild stock. These bred successfully in captivity at first but an increasing infertility led to the ultimate extinction. Another frequently cited example is that of the different stocks of sperm whale. Although taken in total the sperm whale would appear to be quite numerous in the oceans of the world, in certain areas it is clear that specific populations, which do not appear to mix with others, have fallen below the critical point and must be allowed complete peace to regenerate if they are ever to recover.

With wider and still expanding markets for many animal products, and the means of destruction reaching an ever-higher sophistication, the risks of over-exploitation are increasing. In former times so gradual was the change in environment—with a number of startling exceptions—that species were able in time to adapt. This is no longer the case. In this technological age the change is rapid and sometimes drastic. The rorqual whales were virtually immune until the coming of Svend Foyn's explosive harpoon and the steam whale-catcher able to handle a sinking whale. The North American buffalo could survive and provide the Indian with all he needed until the arrival of the railroad and the repeating rifle. In more modern times the addax which was once locally common in the deserts of northern Africa has been almost hunted to extinction by nomads, mining and oil men. Whereas previously the desert fastnesses provided a sanctuary for the addax where he could live undetected and undisturbed, the coming of cross-country vehicles combined with modern weapons has made the animal very vulnerable. Already the addax has almost disappeared from Algeria and Libya. The small Sudanese population is very precarious. Only in the more remote parts of the southern central Sahara and the extreme western Sahara would the addax appear to be holding its own. And for how long?

A similar situation, brought about by the combination of desert-crossing vehicles and modern high-powered weapons, has stripped huge areas of the Arabian peninsula of ground game. So scarce was it in some parts that desert sheiks had to cross the Arabian Gulf in order to find quarry for their falcons. Hunting parties numbering hundreds of vehicles used to sweep in a few hours across distances which would have taken the Bedouin several days or even weeks.

As a result the three species of gazelle which were found in the desert in considerable herds have virtually disappeared, the bustard has become a rarity, and the Arabian oryx—the object of a dramatic rescue operation which made it possible to build up a captive stock for eventual restocking in the wild—became an endangered species.

At first preservation was geared to the continuance of quarry for hunting and sport. In the last century a growing movement was underway to save species for their own sake as being worthy of protection. Later came an awareness that species were interdependent upon one another. But only recently has the realization taken root that what is needed is a full-scale preservation of the ecology of an area—and that the relationships of living species within their physical environments is what really counts. That in fact the ecosystem as a whole rather than individual ingredients had to be preserved.

The destruction of habitat has been continuing for centuries, and in many civilizations—sometimes with devastating results to the civilizations themselves. Thus it is believed that the decline of the Mayan Empire of Central America may have been due to improvident husbandry which led to deforestation and eventual destruction of the soil. Man and his goats virtually destroyed the Mediterranean littoral converting a region of thriving agriculture into barren wastes of desert and naked hills. In the Middle Ages the great forests of western Europe were progressively cleared to satisfy the need for fields and pasture, and timber for ship-building and young industries.

The process is little different now, except that it is taking place at a more alarming rate. In particular excessive grazing is having a devastating effect. In temperate climes the recuperative power of grassland in regions where rainfall is not infrequent enables land to recover comparatively quickly; and the loss is usually temporary. But where rain is scarce in the drier tropical areas the result can be catastrophic and in a matter of a few years grasslands can be converted into moonscapes and once productive savannahs into deserts.

The legacy of this process is a barren wilderness, exposed to every wind that blows and with no protection from the infrequent flashflood which sweeps away what little topsoil the winds have left and causes monumental silting in waterways and estuaries. Artificial regeneration is then rendered almost impossible and prohibitively costly.

Where widespread forest clearance has taken place, the resulting denudation has rendered the soil unstable and led to erosion on a huge scale. This in turn has caused widespread and devastating floods on the lower levels and in the plains. Whereas before the tree complex could absorb some of the immense volume of water accumulated in the mountain regions, and tree and forest roots anchor the soil and prevent landslides, now, with the trees removed, with drainage patterns upset and with the soil open to the elements, the bare rocks act as no more than a slipway for the rains.

It is a different case with the tropical rain forests, which show on an ecological map of the world as a great green girdle astride the Equator (where high temperatures are combined with high rainfall and high humidity). Rain forests hold the richest concentration and diversity of plant and animal life on earth. In an area of a few acres (hectares) as many as 200 different trees may be found—the comparable number in temperate regions would be nearer 20 or 30. And other plant and animal life abounds in astonishing profusion. The rain forests are one of the few wildernesses left on this globe, and they are rapidly disappearing for cattle farming, agricultural use and timber demand. In a number of places the situation is reaching crisis proportions, particularly in New Guinea, the Amazon Basin and parts of West and central Africa and Indonesia.

The rain forest is a highly complex ecological unit. In hot, humid conditions the natural regenerative cycle is rapid. Fallen leaves decay very quickly creating a deeper and deeper layer of humus on which the forest thrives. Within the shelter of the rain forest a predator/prey relationship has evolved which is highly susceptible to disturbance.

If the forestry situation is grave, that of the wetlands is as bad. Marshes, estuaries, bogs and small ponds, inland swamps, fens and low-lying regions of many countries are being drained, reclaimed and converted for agricultural or industrial or building purposes at an alarming rate. These are the breeding grounds of sea bird and waterfowl and fish as well as a host of other species. Each area is a small, balanced community of plant and animal life and cannot be spared.

The conflict between the wants of man and the needs of animals manifests itself in other ways. As an increasing population calls for greater industrialization so its incompatibility with game becomes more apparent and the need for game reserves more pressing. Yet in a number of game reserves a grave imbalance is developing where a too-abundant population of game animals, especially the elephant and the larger herbivores, eats down the available vegetation to an alarming extent. Under these circumstances thinning or culling would seem to be the only practicable answer, yet to many people culling and conservation are incompatible.

The controversy between conservation and culling has raised its head on a number of occasions and will do so on many more. Much of the misunderstanding that has occurred and aroused sometimes over-emotional outcry is due to a failure to realize that conditions have altered. It is a sterile hope that if man discreetly withdrew a natural balance can once again be restored. This is no longer the case for man is now in nearly every instance an essential ingredient in the habitat of those species that come under scrutiny. If man has destroyed the predators which kept the herd in balance, then man must provide an alternative by whatever artificial means he can devise. If the livelihood of industries depends on a natural product and that product is threatened by an over-population of some natural predator the sensible solution would be to thin the predator to manageable size. But by what criteria can 'sensible' be judged? The only valid evidence must be scientific fact and opinion, and in the recent case of the British grey seals, which were saved by the combined efforts of principally the World Wildlife Fund and Greenpeace, culling was suspended until a proper assessment could be made.

Culling, when such culling is justified, can be profitable. The case of the fur seals of the Pribilofs has been cited before. Here by careful management it has been possible to treat the seal population as a crop which can be harvested without detriment to the survival of the species. Even if this cropping, which in the end involves killing and skinning, arouses the emotional wrath of animal lovers, it has been shown that the practice in biological terms has no ill effects on the seal population.

In many other parts of the world game harvesting has been carried on for hundreds of years and with no diminuation of stock. In Iceland the colonies of sea birds were the property of individual farmers or communities and the eggs would be collected only once in each place during the nesting season to allow the birds to lay again and hatch without further interference. Egg collecting has also been a carefully controlled activity for centuries on the Faröe Islands, and murre eggs, which are comparable with hen's eggs in protein content, would be taken without harm to the bird population. Egg collecting is and has been carried on in many other parts of the world, but unless properly managed it has been shown that great harm can be done.

Animal game cropping is becoming increasingly popular and providing a growing source of meat in a number of countries. In the United States the African eland is being herded for its meat. In Africa itself farmers and stock breeders have become aware in the last decades of the potential of native wild animals rather than beef cattle for meat production. In Russia the saving of the Saiga antelope has proved a remarkable success. At one time the Saiga could be found in an immense range in southern Russia and in huge herds but by the latter half of the last century they were declining rapidly under pressure from hide and meat hunters. Despite prohibitions placed on the killing of the animal in 1919, by 1930 there were only 1,000 left and these were widely scattered in small populations. As a result of careful management however, the Saiga can now be numbered in millions and an annual harvest taken without impairing the animal's future.

Ironically, the encouragement of interest in wildlife can have a paradoxically detrimental effect. In Snowdonia in Wales, so populated is the region in summer that the constant passing of climbers, walkers and tourists is turning simple tracks into well-worn highways and destroying much of the natural beauty of the place. In Poland, where the Bialowieza Forest, bounding the Russian border and the home of the last wild herd of the European bison (an animal which once roamed the forests of much of the continent and is now a herd some 200 strong) another threat emerged recently, an outbreak of foot and mouth disease in nearby Czechoslovakia which could have wiped out the entire species. As a result it was necessary to stop the annual 100,000 visitors to the park from viewing the bison.

The arrival of the chemical age has led to grave threats to the survival of many species and horrifying instances have been brought to public notice in a host of countries. Seabirds and pollution make ready news. Disasters to such ocean giants as the *Amoco Cadiz*, the *Christos Bitas* and the *Eleni V* which have led to huge oil slicks and the deaths of countless sea birds are well advertized occasions, but there are many lesser ones not large enough or too local to attract international attention. None the less these are enough to create havoc and untold damage to sea bird populations, and it is sometimes forgotten that although sea birds are often washed ashore fouled with oil, vast numbers more having their buoyancy destroyed sink at sea. If by some unhappy chance oil spillage should occur near the site of some sea bird already threatened and with reduced or reducing population the new menace could be decisive. Thus a comparatively small spillage in Sullom Voe in the Shetland Islands in December 1978 could prove a very severe blow to the Great

Northern Diver. With no sign of a reduction of sea traffic, the threats to sea birds from oil pollution is likely to mount rather than recede. And those coasts near active sealanes, such as those along the East Coast of Britain and the west coast of Europe, the Baltic coasts and parts of the Mediterranean are particularly vulnerable.

The unwise importation of species has had a catastrophic effect on indigenous wildlife in many parts of the world. The tale of the rabbit in Australia is well-known, but other importations have had as drastic repercussions. That of the mongoose, brought in to counter rats in the sugar plantations has been nothing short of disastrous. In the islands of Barbados, Jamaica, Cuba, St Vincent, St Lucia, Trinidad, Nevis in the West Indies and Fiji and Hawaii in the Pacific, the mongoose became a menace, for the imported species took to consuming anything and everything. Birds, pigs, kids and domestic fowl all fell prey to the mongoose in Hawaii, and there it developed a sweet tooth and even took to eating the sugar cane it was brought in to protect.

Natural predator/prey relationships are tampered with at peril. The onslaught on hawks and owls and the bounty placed on them which some unwise state authorities imposed at the end of the last century, led to a virtual plague of rats and mice in fields and agricultural holdings. The wholesale war on wolves in Canada was followed by a serious deterioration in the quality of caribou herds. Whereas formerly the sick and weakly would be culled by this natural means, now there were too few wolves to carry out this necessary natural purging, with the inevitable result. If these are straightforward instances there are others more obscure, for the complex relationships inherent in an environment are only just beginning to be understood, and much is still clearly unknown.

The leopard is becoming increasingly scarce. Leopard heads in an East African market some years ago.

The poisoning of bait for vermin has resulted in tragic loss of hawks, eagles and vultures. DDT and Dieldrin and other persistent poisons accumulate in the bodies of animals and as the natural cycle of predator and prey takes its course so they are passed on. A strong dose can cause death, a weaker dose a loss in fertility or sometimes weakened egg shells which crack in the nest under the parents' weight. As many of these birds are also the target for egg collectors a number of raptor species are particularly vulnerable.

Perhaps most damaging of all are the commercial sales of the products of many species, be it polished turtle shells, songbird paté, or the skins of spotted cats. Legislators will legislate—and the International Union for the Conservation of Nature and Natural Resources (IUCN) recently played a major role in formulating the Convention on International Trade in Endangered Species of Wild Fauna and Flora (CITES)—which will do a great deal to save species threatened by trade. But as long as a market still exists for these goods, the sale, legal or illicit, will continue. Someone, somewhere will always want the skin of a leopard and as long as the price obtainable is equivalent to or more than the entire annual earnings of the hunter—as is the case in many parts of the world—so the depredations and widespread poaching will continue. From our own position of comfortable self-righteousness we can condemn such activities as wanton, yet they are not so far removed from those practised against the animal world by Europeans in the last and earlier decades of the present century. And with considerably less justification.

The hunter today is one of wildlife's lesser threats. Although the hunter himself is subject to the complex and ambivalent attitudes of his sport, in many ways he is the greatest conservationist of all, albeit perhaps to the conservation purist for the wrong reasons. To many people hunting is a fundamental way of life rather than a sport. Many hunters if asked would call themselves game-watchers rather than game-slayers. In the world we have created for ourselves the hunter has now become an important part in the scheme of things—he has taken the place of the natural predator.

The threats to wildlife today are manifold and various. Conservationists have a long and occasionally bitter road to travel. Sometimes their efforts will fail and a long-cherished species will just cease to exist; sometimes their efforts, particularly at educating another generation to the true meaning of their wildlife heritage, will be successful. But the pressing need is, as it has been since man first strode this planet, to find a reconciliation with the wildlife around him. Whether he is succeeding and succeeding quickly enough is more obscure.

For the bare statistics in a recent World Conservation Strategy published by the IUCN makes frightening reading. It is estimated for instance that at current rates one third of the world's land suitable for growing crops will be lost before the end of the century. That the present state of over-fishing in the world's oceans has already meant a reduced catch of one tenth, and that this figure will increase. That 40 per cent of the world's original rain forest has already been destroyed and that we are felling and clearing at the rate of 30 hectares every minute. That one fifth of the globe's entire land surface is threatened with being turned into desert. And that as a result of these encroachments and many more both direct and indirect, more than 1,000 animals and over 25,000 plant species are faced with extinction. If man's toll has been enormous in the past, the potential catastrophe to very many species in the future would appear to be vastly greater.

As Sir Peter Scott has said, 'Leopard skins look better on leopards'.

A New Enlightenment?

Animals are our fellow brethren, in suffering, disease and death.

Charles Darwin, *Origin of Species*

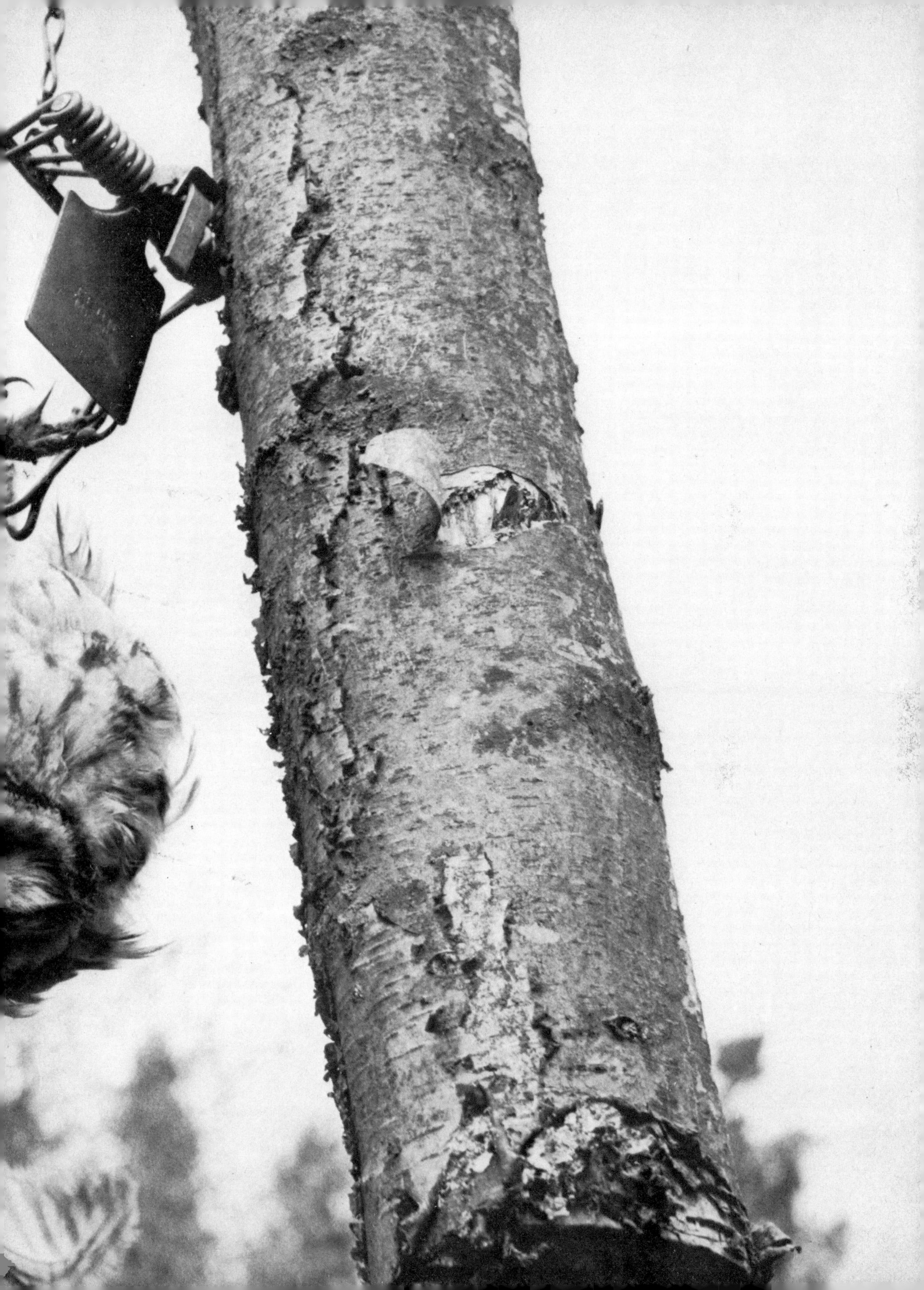

(Previous pages) A Long-eared owl in a pole trap. Although illegal killing accounts for many birds, loss of habitat is now the principal danger for many species.

The decisive change in the moral attitude of man towards animals started in the latter half of the last century, and if this was not wholly, it was very largely due to the publication of Darwin's *Origin of Species* in 1859. With it men began to look differently at the natural world. No longer as a collection of separate species, entities in themselves and derived from no common ancestor, but as a 'web of life' interdependent on each other. This was a direct attack at the literal interpretation of the Scriptures and in particular on the supremacy of man over animals which the verses of Genesis had made so clear. It was the start of a movement which was to take the civilized world by storm and to overturn longstanding ideas not only of nature and man's relationship with nature, but of man's inherent superiority over the animal kingdom and the creatures of the world.

Darwin's work emerged at a time of great stirring in the western nations. Fuelled by a huge population increase in Europe and the United States, it was an age of revolution. Political revolution in a number of countries, but also a revolution of thought. For the rumblings of democracy and socialism were already being felt; invention, education and industry were on the march. There was a new liberalism abroad, and a detectable class restlessness which was to assail many preconceived concepts and conventional opinions. The language of this new age was science.

As Thomas Henry Huxley, Darwin's 'Bulldog' as he called himself, strode the country preaching the new Darwinian theories he met with an astonishing response. Whereas at first he was greeted by learned and philosophical societies with polite applause, scepticism and, occasionally, with downright hostility, with working men's audiences he aroused an amazing reaction. By bewitching oratory he made science comprehensible to the ordinary man. His exposition, and the clarity of his approach had an evangelical effect—listeners would write to him afterwards to say that they had just enjoyed the most moving experience of their lives.

Yet this new philosophy was a direct challenge to the social, religious and moral foundations which surrounded them. Evolution meant low origins, and Victorian England was nothing if not proud of its origins. Further, since if any suggestion of the common origin of man and brute questioned the account of creation given by the Bible which for so long had been taken as a biological and geological treatise, this 'brutal philosophy' was a clear denial of the Scriptures. But in many circles there was already a vacuum of faith, and a resentment at the power and privilege of the Church. Many needed a new god, and the new god was science. Science was a liberation, a solace, a passport to salvation and a better lot. The result was a thirsting for knowledge of all sorts.

To the animal world the effects of the *Origin of Species* was far-reaching. People began to look at animals in a different light—after all poke a monkey with a stick and you could be poking a distant relative.

Man himself was already being set free. On 31 July 1834, in the 'greatest adventure in humanity', 800,000 slaves in the British colonies were freed. The American Civil War accelerated the process and across the world a burgeoning restlessness for emancipation began to make its presence felt, a search for human dignity was under way and with it the first promise that democracy for man ought to lead to freedom for beasts.

There had been many stirrings in the zoological sciences over previous centuries, but the mid-eighteenth century saw the most significant advances. Then Carolus Linnaeus (1707–78) had pioneered a new classification of species and Comte de Buffon, born in the same year as Linnaeus, but who survived for a decade after the great Swede, undertook similar work in comparative anatomy. Others in many lands added to the growing sum of natural knowledge—and not a few helped to confuse the situation utterly. A milestone was Sir Charles Lyell's *Elements of Geology*, which was to set in motion the proper study of that science, establish a foundation from which a mass of other knowledge could derive and fire the first shots in the coming war between the 'new science' and orthodoxy.

In the natural sciences this interest flowered in exhibits at zoos, museums and menageries. These and teaching at schools created a widening knowledge of natural history and a growing interest in 'Nature'. Darwinianism, the heretical and revolutionary proposition was, within 20 years, 'a fact no rational man could dispute'. Across the civilized world it had radically changed man's approach to natural life.

In Britain the anatomical genius of the artist George Stubbs (1724–1806), the drawings of Thomas Bewick and the art of Landseer; the activities of the Royal Society for the Prevention of Cruelty to Animals (founded in 1824 and given Royal status in 1840) along with other organizations and bodies—helped to give credence to the growing conception that animals had 'rights' and that nature had a place in the order of things and had sometimes to be protected.

In America the works of Alexander Wilson and, later Audubon, that of the artist/explorer George Catlin (illustrator of animals and the Indians of the American West), the writings of Henry David Thoreau, Ralph Waldo Emerson, George Perkins Marsh and, later of John Burroughs and many others, brought 'Nature' home to people and showed how precious and fragile a heritage it was.

Already there was a detectable divergence of approach on the two sides of the Atlantic. British and to a lesser extent European conservationism, as the movement came to be called, leaned more on the concept of the animal as an individual. If he needed protection from man's improvidence and ravages then he must be protected and if that protection meant sealing off an area from incursion then that area must be sealed off. To the American however, Nature was the prime consideration. The huge untouched areas of their immense country, public land rather than private as pertained in Britain and parts of Europe, needed to be preserved from the encroachments of industrial development and the savagery of progress. It was desirable to maintain stocks of the indigenous wildlife within these areas as part of the general scene, but the principal consideration was the preservation of the wildness. These divergences disappeared during the early years of the present century. But at the outset when the birth pains of conservationism were being felt on both sides of the Atlantic and opposed by vested commercial interests of all sorts, they heavily coloured the approach to the problem.

The aftermath of the American Civil War and the early 1870s were heady days in the history of the growth of conservationist movements. The advent of the steam-powered press meant that at last cheap literature could be obtained; magazines of all sorts flourished, particularly children's magazines. In the United States the churches took a lead in championing the preservation of Nature in its broadest form, and 'Bird Days', days set aside for the study of birds, became a common feature in American school curricula. And a number of works which invoked at one and the same time the beauty and the fragility of nature became popular reading. None more so than Thoreau's *Walden*, which had been first published as long before as 1854. In it he wrote:

> We need the tonic of wildness—to wade sometimes in marshes where the bittern and the meadow-hen lurk, and hear the booming of the snipe, to smell the whispering sedge where only some wilder and more solitary fowl builds her nest, and the mink crawls with its belly close to the ground. At the same time that we are earnest to explore and learn all things, we require that all things be mysterious and unexplorable, that land and sea be infinitely wild, unsurveyed, and unfathomed by us because unfathomable. We can never have enough of Nature.

This intellectual and emotional dawning coincided with some of the worst plunderings of the animal world that ever took place. The 1870s were to see the start of the slaughter of the North American buffalo, and the continuing killing of the fur seals in their thousands in the North Pacific. The great plumage war was about to reach its height, and in Africa the once vast stocks of old ivory had all but been used up and the first dramatic inroads into the elephant population about to be made. Across the world and in many different commodities animal stocks were being decimated to satisfy the commercial interests of growing industrial power, and its attendant needs for food and finery.

The voices against such a waste of animal resources, a hunt so often accompanied by great cruelty, grew in volume. Societies were formed, particularly in Britain and the United States, and in the latter natural reservations were created.

Poisoning and pollution have reduced the populations of many birds of prey. This is a white-tailed sea eagle.

There had been murmurings urging the establishment of natural reservations in the United States for many years. As early as 1833 Catlin had written:

> These regions [referring to the west] might in future be seen by some great policy of government preserved in their pristine beauty and wildness, in a magnificent park, where the world could see for ages to come, the native Indian in his classic attire, galloping his wild horse ... amid the fleeting herds of elks and buffaloes. What a beautiful and thrilling specimen for America to preserve and hold up to the view of her refined citizens and the world, in future ages. A nation's Park containing man and beast, in all the wild and freshness of their nature's beauty.

Emerson had sought much the same and urged people to look on Nature with 'new eyes', and later he wrote that the 'interminable forests should become graceful parks for use and for delight'. By the early 1850s artists and writers of considerable persuasion had begun to penetrate the northern states and told of and depicted the grandeur of the scenery. Magazines such as *Harper's Weekly*, founded in 1850 (and the *Atlantic Monthly* seven years later), devoted many articles on nature and its preservation. Thus when the grandeur and wonders of the incredible Yosemite Valley and the great Sequoia groves of California were discovered, and later photographed, the American public were fast becoming aware of their unique natural heritage.

In 1864 the Yosemite Valley and the nearby Mariposa Big Tree Grove was preserved, first as a state park and subsequently as a national park. The first national park though, was Yellowstone, created in March 1872 'as a public park and pleasuring ground for the benefit and enjoyment of the people'.

The craving for 'wilderness', for sanctuary from the oppressions of urban life and a world becoming harshly industrial proved compelling to many Americans. A growing number of people found a pleasure, often a necessity, to commune with nature. 'A party spent two pleasant weeks in the summer of 1873 in eating, sleeping, rollicking, and trout fishing in the wilderness of Northern New York, to the great benefit of their physical being and without harm to their souls or interference with the rights or enjoyment of their fellow men,' wrote a correspondent in *Forest and Stream*, a magazine which punched home the message that more than half the pleasure of sport was the natural surroundings in which it was partaken.

A principal disciple in the ways and virtues of 'Nature' was William T. Hornaday, in 1887 chief taxidermist to the United States National Museum who was a pioneer conservationist. He wrote 'We are weary of witnessing the greed, selfishness and cruelty of "Civilised" man towards the wild creatures of the earth. We are sick of tales of slaughter and pictures of carnage.'

The most distinguished of the growing band of conservationists in America was President Theodore Roosevelt. A noted big game shot, he spent a large proportion of his life in hunting, especially as a young man. When shortly after giving up the presidency in 1909 he set forth on a widely publicized safari to East Africa where in the interests of 'scientific purposes' he accounted for over 200 head of game. Yet almost single-handed he was to set the United States on the course of conservation which prevails today. The early national parks and reserves as well as the policy behind them owe their origin to the enthusiasm and far-sighted idealism of this one man who declared that he was 'not building this country of ours for a day, but, to last through the ages.'

A principal concern at this time was the wasting of American forest resources. Of an original 800 million acres of virgin forest when the Pilgrim Fathers landed, less than 200 million remained. And this was being whittled away on a gigantic scale to make way for agricultural settlement. Already unrestricted and improvident grazing by huge heads of livestock was turning thousands of acres of once fertile land into barren desert, open now to the erosion of wind, weather and time. By 1900 it was clear that a radical new policy was needed in the United States to counter the trend of disappearing natural resources. In 1902 a water reclamation act was passed. Between 1902 and 1910 five national parks were created—at Crater Lake, Oregon; Wind Cave, South Dakota; Platt, Oklahoma; Sully Hill, North Dakota; and Mesa Verde in Colorado. In 1908 Roosevelt arranged for a Conservation Committee to be established to assess natural resources. This was followed in 1909 by a National Conservation Conference and there were plans for a first world conference on natural resources, but the project lapsed when Roosevelt ceased to be president.

But in 1916, as perhaps the crowning culmination of all these efforts, the National Park Service was founded in America to 'conserve the scenery and the natural and historic objects and wildlife therein, and to provide for the enjoyment of the same in such a manner and by such means as will leave them unimpaired for the enjoyment of future generations'.

This was pioneering work, for the rest of the world was considerably more backward, although individual countries had set up national parks before the turn of the century. Thus in Canada, in 1885, Rocky

The walrus, once hunted for its tusks in an Arctic nature reserve.

Mountain park was established (it was later named Banff), and was followed by two others before the turn of the century, while in 1911 a Park Service was established. 1891 had already seen created a park in Belair in Australia. Three years later came one in New Zealand and the Pongola reserve in South Africa—which was later deproclaimed. 1898 saw the setting up of what is probably the most famous game reserve in the world, the Kruger National Park, in the Eastern Transvaal,

The koala bear was once almost hunted to extinction for its fur.

originally known as the Sabi Game Reserve and renamed in honour of its far-sighted instigator and protagonist President Paul Kruger.

In Europe the national park movement was slow to start, but once begun it quickly gathered momentum and started to assume growing importance as wildlife sanctuaries. In 1914 the Swiss National Park was created. In 1922 the Gran Paradiso, in Italy, formerly a royal hunting park, which was almost the last home in the Alps of the Ibex. In 1928 perhaps the most famous of all European national parks, the Camargue Reserve in southern France, was set up. Britain, although a pioneer in the general conservationist campaigns, was slow to coordinate conservationist activities. In 1912 the Society for the Promotion of Nature Reserves was founded and looked after a number of nature reserves. Now, as the Society for the Promotion of Nature Conservation, it acts as the umbrella organisation for the care of over 1,000 nature reserves of varying sizes.

The conservation movement has travelled far since those days, and is now a world spanning international hydra with many heads. It was in the world of the birds that the first truly international developments were seen. The early trans-national ornithological conferences in Vienna in 1868, Vienna again in 1884 and elsewhere in later years flowered into an International Committee for Bird Preservation in 1922 (later the name was changed to the International Council for Bird Preservation, ICBP). In the animal world the Society for the Preservation of the Wild Fauna of the Empire, which was to become in 1950 the Fauna Preservation Society was founded in 1903. On a wider platform just before the Second World War the International Office for the Protection of Nature was founded in Brussels. In 1948 at Fontainbleau this was renamed as the International Union which, in 1956, became the existing International Union for Conservation of Nature and Natural Reserves and, in 1961 gave birth to its fund-raising sister organization, the World Wildlife Fund.

The activities of these and many other domestic and specialized conservation organizations have had a resounding effect on protecting our natural heritage by changing legislation, buying land and educating the public to wildlife needs. But the overall concern still remains the reconciliation of man with his natural surroundings. And it is not just a question of preserving what is there, putting it in cold store and forgetting about it; such hopes today are foredoomed. Man's needs are not going to remain static. His population is going to increase and with it his need for more food.

He will need more land for industry and development and, as the technological revolution proceeds, so there will be greater need for areas for relaxation, for sport and for the growing leisure he will be burdened with. But his crying need will always be to find and maintain the new harmony between his own needs and those of the nature he seeks to preserve—and these requirements are often conflicting. This will need comprehension—which means research—and it will need widespread education of the true appreciation of natural surroundings and man's place within them. The goal must be to stop man's excessive exploitation and plundering of Nature, but not to forbid or prevent—if such prohibition or prevention were possible—the sensible use of his environment for his needs. He must find a balance between his own needs and those that Nature can provide without detriment, either to population or environment.

Many of the tales in these chapters have revealed astonishing wantonness, but it has also revealed a state of total ignorance of what was happening. Had communications been better, had the big-game hunters been aware of how African game was being annihilated, the fore-runner of the Fauna Preservation Society would perhaps have been born 20 years earlier. But communications were almost non-existent, information of what was happening was tardy and often inaccurate. Only a gradual awareness of the true state of affairs from their fellow hunters, and their own experiences, told the founder members of the Fauna Preservation Society that something decisive and probably irreversible was occurring to the game in Africa that had provided so many pleasurable hours to them and their fellows. No hunting man or sportsman worthy of the name would hunt to extermination, their fault was more one of ignorance rather than callousness.

No such excuse is permissible today.

Will he and many other species survive for the future? A harpy eagle in a nature reserve in Surinam.

Acknowledgements

Very many people have helped me with the preparation of this book, but I would like to make special mention of the Hudson's Bay Company and especially Mr Hugh Dwan; the Royal Society for the Protection of Birds; Greenpeace and the World Wildlife Fund, in particular Janet Barber of the WWF for a wealth of valuable advice and suggestions. Also to Michael Stephenson, my editor, whose idea this book was and whose skilled midwifery has brought it into the world.

Picture Credits

The author and publishers would like to thank the following for supplying illustrations.

	Page
Aerpix Press	129, 130
Mary Evans Picture Library	158
Hudson's Bay Company	47
Illustrated London News	24, 94
Illustrated Sporting and Dramatic News	104, 105
Mansell Collection	9, 16, 30, 36/37, 39, 42, 50/51, 68/69, 86, 87, 90/91, 96, 102, 108, 110, 112, 114, 132/33, 139, 146
North Dakota Game and Fish Department	
(Frank A. Johnson Museum, Fullerton)	10/11
(H. O. Odegard, Heimdal)	148
(Osborne Studio, Dickinson)	77, 145
Novosti Press Agency	44, 181
Radio Times Hulton Picture Library	17, 20, 21, 23, 32, 33, 46, 55, 56, 89, 93, 119, 120, 153, 154, 161
The Royal Society for the Protection of Birds	
(P. Merrin)	174
(R. Porter)	131
World Wildlife Fund	54, 57t, 59, 97, 109, 123, 173, 182
(Bengtsson)	179
(Dr. B. Grzimek)	172
(Douglas Hamilton)	100
(Kenya Information Service)	98/99
(Richard Orr)	57b
(D. Paterson)	117
(Puchalski)	2/3 and 190/91
(Dr J. P. Schulz)	185
(Uri Tzon)	164/65
(Dr F. K. Zeller)	34
(Christian Zuber)	162
Yellowstone National Park	76

(Overleaf) Saved from extinction—two cow European bison with their young.

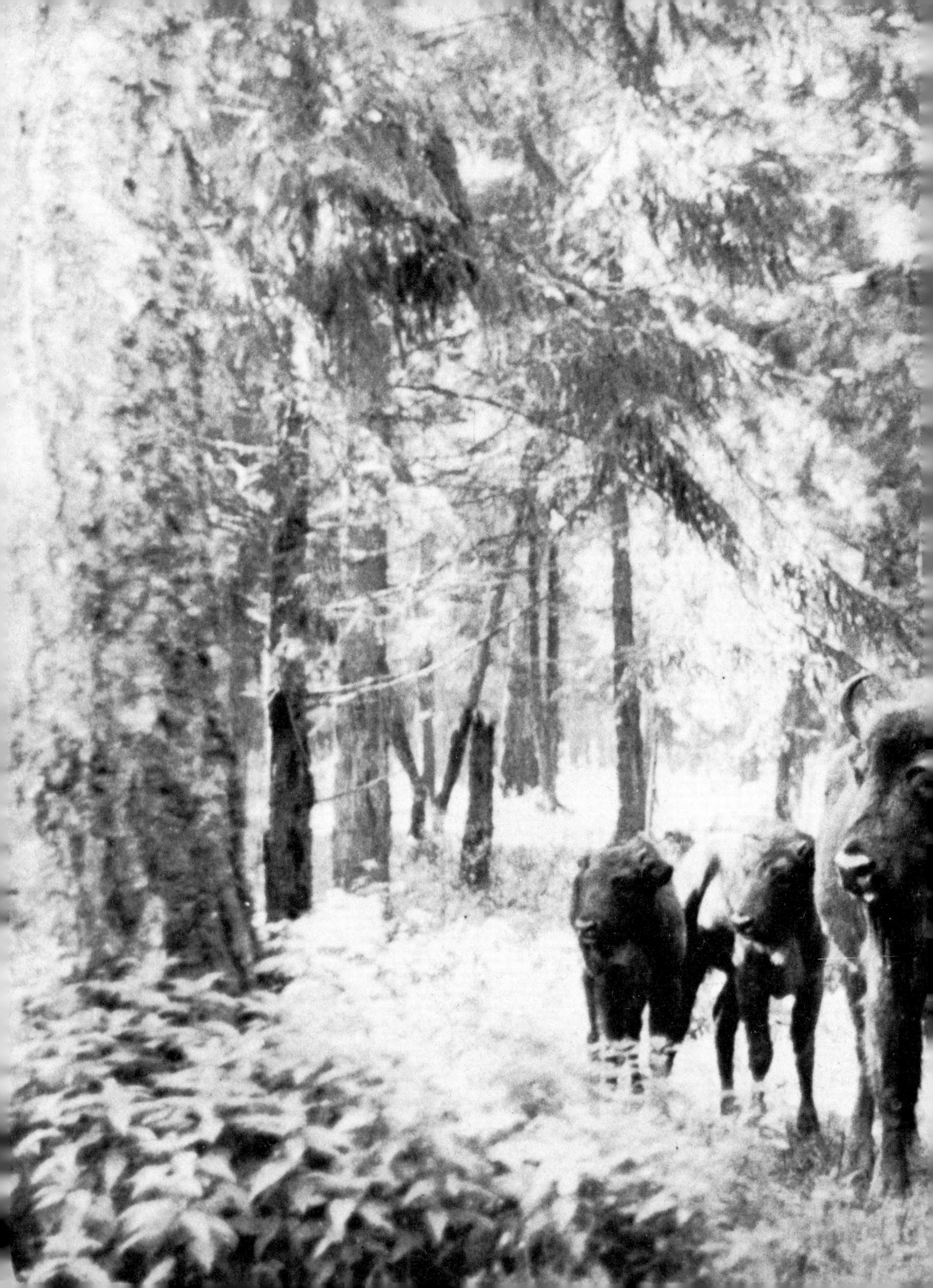